FAMINE, CONFLICT AND RESPONSE

FAMINE, CONFLICT AND RESPONSE

A BASIC GUIDE

Frederick C. Cuny

with

Richard B. Hill

KUMARIAN
PRESS

Famine, Conflict and Response: A Basic Guide

Published 1999 in the United States of America by Kumarian Press, Inc.,
14 Oakwood Avenue, West Hartford, Connecticut 06119-2127 USA

Production and design by The Sarov Press, Stratford, Connecticut.
Graphics by Evolve Productions.
Index by L. Pilar Wyman.
The text of this book is set in 10/13 Adobe Sabon.

Printed in Canada on acid-free paper by
Transcontinental Printing and Graphics, Inc.
Text printed with vegetable oil-based ink.

∞ The paper used in this publication meets the minimum requirements
of the American National Standard for Information Sciences—Permanence of
Paper for Printed Library Materials, ANSI Z39.48–1984.

Library of Congress Cataloging-in-Publication Data
Cuny, Frederick C.
      Famine, conflict and response : a basic guide / by Frederick C. Cuny ;
with Richard B. Hill.
            p.   cm.
      Includes bibliographical references and index.
      ISBN 1–56549–090–8 (pbk. : alk. paper)
      1. Food relief. 2. War relief. 3. Famines. I. Hill, Richard B. II. Title.
HV696.F6C86 1999
363.8'83—dc21   98–49090

03   02   01   00   99   5   4   3   2   1   First Printing 1999

Contents

List of Illustrations

Publisher's Note

Fred Cuny was a passionate humanitarian who disappeared under mysterious circumstances in Chechnya. During his extraordinary career he helped thousands of people worldwide. Governments and organizations that work to relieve suffering caused by disasters and conflict will continue to be influenced by Cuny's legacy.

Kumarian Press wishes to thank two key people who assisted in making Fred Cuny's writing on famine available to the world. Rick Hill, Fred Cuny's colleague, helped make this book a reality with his skilled input and knowledge of the field. His persistent dedication to seeing that this book would be published led to the publication of this seminal work on famine relief and prevention. Thanks go also to the editor of this book, Pat Reed, who did the hard work of polishing and editing the manuscript while working from Bosnia-Herzegovina. Her skill as an editor enabled Fred Cuny, her friend and colleague, to share his innovative ideas and experience in famine relief with all who devote themselves to people in need, anywhere in the world. We are most grateful to Rick Hill and Pat Reed.

PHOTO BY RICHARD B. HILL

Fred Cuny (second from right) and colleagues in Bangladesh coordinating the building of cyclone shelters after the devastating cyclone of 1991.

Preface

I met Fred Cuny in the 1960s, long before he became one of the visionaries in the disaster-management world. I was a newspaper reporter in Houston, Texas, who had been assigned to cover a civil rights demonstration against a local elementary school principals association that still remained segregated. A national principals association, of which the local was a member, was holding its annual convention in the city, and Fred was the leader of the demonstration. While talking to him, I discovered we had gone to the same high school in Dallas. At the time, we were both married, and our families quickly became friends.

Fred eventually started doing disaster management, and I kept up with him sporadically, receiving an occasional letter or card. Sometimes he dropped in for a few days to visit.

In 1990, bored with American journalism, I went to work for Fred. He was a fascinating guy to have as your employer. Most of the time, he simply gave you your assignment and then he left the region, off doing other things. You'd be in southern Iraq; he was in northern Iraq. You'd be in Bosnia-Herzegovina; he'd have headed to Washington, D.C., talking to the government, trying to convince people to change the way they were handling the war in Bosnia. Sometimes you'd wish desperately that he were still around so you could talk to him about *exactly* what it was he wanted you to do. When he returned, he either liked your work or hated it.

In my early days with him, he passed me off as being far more experienced than I was. When the United Nations Development Programme Emergency Unit in Sudan was considering me for a job as its information officer, he told the organization I had won the Pulitzer Prize. Of course, I hadn't, but they offered me the job anyway. After the Persian Gulf War was over and displaced Iraqis had gathered in the southern part of that country, he let the U.S. Army believe I was an expert on refugees when Intertect, Fred's company, was hired to help them run the refugee camp. I had never seen a refugee in my life.

I began in 1990 to edit the vast number of papers Fred had written over the years—an assignment I had considerably more experience doing.

Fred was a prolific writer. Every time he had a few minutes, he wrote a paper on something in the disaster world. Sometimes his papers were simple; often, they were significantly more complicated. In Bosnia, for example, he spent a serious amount of time putting together a briefing book on the history of the country, the reasons for the war, and the international community's response to it. He believed—correctly—that most humanitarians and military personnel arrived in a country at war with little, if any, good information on the situation. His Bosnia briefing book was a phenomenal accomplishment, and he handed it out to almost anyone who expressed interest—and probably some who didn't.

Fred had begun working on a book on famine in the 1980s. He finished one version a number of years ago and gave it to me to edit. After I edited the book, however, Fred decided he wanted to rewrite it, working on a new version off and on for several years. In 1992, while in Somalia, he asked Rick Hill, the number two person at Intertect, Fred's disaster management company, to contribute significantly to the parts of the book that dealt with monetization and market-based interventions. After Fred disappeared in Chechnya in 1995 (he is now presumed dead), Rick Hill added major sections to the book, clarified others, and refined the overall effort. Rick is also responsible for much of the illustrative material that accompanies *Famine, Conflict and Response: A Basic Guide.*

When Fred disappeared, he left no record of the people he had talked to concerning this book. However, Andrew Natsios, Mike Viola, Gayle Smith, Paul Thompson, Barbara Hendrie, Mike Toole, Alicia Acosta, Alex Rondos, Peter Walker, the Disaster Management Center in Madison, Wisconsin, Rick Hill, and others contributed greatly to it. Thanks also go to the many relief workers and planners who—through long discussions in the field and back in the office—contributed to Fred and Rick's understanding of famine.

Special thanks go to the John D. and Catherine T. MacArthur Foundation, which gave me a grant to edit this book and two others. (The foundation had named Fred as one of its MacArthur Fellows in 1995, not long after he disappeared in Chechnya.) In addition, the Feinstein International Famine Center of Tufts University and World Vision provided much-needed assistance in getting this primer published. (Rick Hill did a fantastic job arranging this assistance.) The Center for the Study of Societies in Crisis, the nonprofit organization Fred put together in the 1980s, also played a major role in the publication of this book, particularly in seeking the MacArthur grant.

PAT REED

Introduction

By John C. Hammock and Andrew Natsios

Fred Cuny was a unique phenomenon in the humanitarian-relief community: the ultimate field worker who was also a scholar and intellectual. Fred participated at some level in the response to many of the greatest disasters in the 1980s and 1990s until his untimely death in Chechnya in 1995. From the Ethiopian and Sudanese droughts to the gulf war and the Kurdish emergency in Northern Iraq and from Bosnia to Chechnya, Fred was present at the inception and gave advice to whoever listened as well as designed and carried out programs under extraordinarily difficult circumstances. His powers of observation and analysis were his greatest strengths, allowing him to aggregate disparate and seemingly unrelated data into a coherent explanation of what was happening and then design a comprehensive strategy to address the crisis.

His analyses, including those in this book, showed the mind of a preeminent economist of disasters. Fred constantly returned to economic principles to explain events. For him, politics, military strategy, economics, and humanitarian relief were not unrelated sectors divorced from each other, but rather intimately connected, playing off one another in sometimes insidious and unintended ways. He used these same economists' tools in writing this book on famine and how to deal with it in a practical and understandable way. Whenever Fred traveled to a food emergency, he would first stop at the local market to review prices for grain and livestock and to talk with merchants about inflationary pressures, the volume of commodity turnover in the market, the sources of commodity supply, and what local ethnic or political groups the merchants were allied with. And then he would simply stand and observe: who was buying, what they were buying, and what they were using for currency. By the end of the first day, he would understand much of the economy of famine in the region. The rest of his assessment would prove or disprove his initial hypotheses, and he would adjust his analysis as he collected more data.

One of the traditional weaknesses of humanitarian agencies has been their inability to be reflective and undertake objective analysis of their relief response at a more strategic level. This void is usually filled by scholars who have little practical field experience in famines—a fact that makes their conclusions sometimes suspect. For more than a decade and a half, Fred Cuny methodically recorded all of his experiences and observations in case studies and reports which capture lessons learned for the next disaster response. If disaster responses have improved during this period, Fred and his prodigious writing must be given some of the credit. Perhaps his great, lasting contribution to the education of the current crop of humanitarian-relief managers was his drafting (with a group of associates) of the early curriculum for the Disaster Management Center at the University of Wisconsin, through which thousands of relief workers have been trained.

A particularly humorous incident took place during the Kurdish emergency. Fred, a consultant to the Office of Foreign Disaster Assistance in the United States Agency for International Development, was having a particularly animated argument with an official of the United Nations High Commissioner for Refugees (UNHCR) about the design of refugee camps. Fred quoted the UNHCR manual on camp construction and management at some length to the UNHCR officer from memory, by page number. The skeptical UN officer demanded to know how Fred could remember so much from the manual, doubting his accuracy. Fred replied: "I wrote the manual." That ended the argument.

All of Cuny's arguments did not end so easily, with Fred winning the day. His great weakness was his inability—his refusal might be a more accurate word—to manage the bureaucratic and organizational politics of the institutions he sometimes tried to work through. He had no patience for it, yet without political-management skills, his ability to move troglodyte organizational structures and relief managers wedded to old relief practices was sometimes limited. Fred's reputation as a rebel was derived, in part, from his frustration in trying to force the large and complex institutions he worked with to do what he knew was right (and he usually was).

Fred had a fertile mind, reflected in the invention and ingenuity of the analysis in this book. He was an extraordinary innovator in virtually every discipline of disaster response, from his early work in natural disasters, particularly earthquakes and storms, to his final work on wars and famines.

Fred left a legacy of ideas and written work. From his first interventions, Fred had a clear sense of what worked and what did not. In his first major work, *Disasters and Development*, Fred outlined his thinking. It is from this initial work that the following principles for effective work in humanitarian assistance can be summarized:

The context of the emergency is crucial. Emergencies cannot be viewed as separate from local politics or economics. He stated, "for them [the government] control of disaster response cannot be separated from politics." In every disaster, there are winners and losers, people who gain and people who are worse off. Clearly, the people hit worst are the poor. For Fred, poverty was the primary root cause of the vulnerability of people, and sending food, blankets, and traditional forms of assistance could not be done in a vacuum but had to be seen as impacting the economics, politics, and development of a region.

Traditional responses by international agencies can cause more harm than good. Fred felt that international agencies had simplistic ideas of aid, ideas that assumed the best solutions came from overseas. He cautioned that international aid agencies must "re-examine [their] underlying assumptions about disasters and how people react . . . and about the nature of the organizations that have been established to respond." His criticism of agencies was harsh: "Most agencies are still focusing on emergency needs, and few fully understand the events that occur in a disaster and how their intervention affects the overall outcome of recovery."

International aid is a drop in the bucket compared with local aid. He wrote: "International aid is highly visible, yet it represents only a small part of the total recovery picture, both in terms of resources and the actions taking place within the affected society." This realization places international aid in perspective and should teach relief agencies humility and to look at what local people are doing.

The key to success in relief aid is involving local people directly. Fred was an active listener. He believed in communicating directly with people who have been affected by emergencies. He knew that victims of disasters are not helpless. He urged using the word *participant*, not victim. He urged that "decision making be locally based, not transferred to Geneva, New York, or Nairobi." He knew that local people understood their situation best and that response mechanisms needed to be built on local skills and knowledge. "[Good] programs not only stressed local decision making and involvement, but further reinforced the existing community structures (coping mechanisms) . . . ." In fact, he tried to dispel three myths about the behavior of victims: that victims are helpless; that disasters require outside assistance for the victims to cope; and that disasters wipe out indigenous coping mechanisms.

Relief and development are intricately linked. Fred wrote, "The basic problem was the conceptual failure by aid organizations to link disasters and development . . . . The relief agencies tended to view disasters solely as emergencies. This meant that the best way to respond was by providing emergency medical assistance, basic goods, and temporary emergency shelter." And for Fred, this was shortsighted and often wrong. Fred believed emergencies were a time ripe for change in long-term economic and political structures. Issues of land tendency and relationships among economic and social classes were disturbed by emergencies and offered an opportunity for social and economic change. He also saw that it was not just relief that had an impact on development but also that development impacted disaster response. Unfortunately, not many agencies heeded his prediction: "Many agencies, especially those involved in both relief and development, will complete the circle, realizing that the connections between disasters and development also run in the other direction (that is, development to disasters)."

Relief aid is not a logistical exercise to get goods to people—it is a process to accelerate recovery. Fred criticized relief efforts that viewed their work as a tactical or logistics problem. He emphasized that effective relief took into account the process that the local community was going through. "By failing to understand the elements of each community activity and their interrelationships, an outsider may respond inappropriately and delay or prevent a return to normal."

Relief intervention teaches us lessons; we should heed the lessons learned from the past. Fred listed a series of lessons he had learned by the early 1980s. These included, among others not mentioned above: that relief and reconstruction operations should be conducted within the context of development; that people can do it and they know how; that people consistently prefer private and informal solutions over public and formal ones; that activities should be appropriate to the phase of the disaster; that massive relief can be counterproductive; that the anticipation of large-scale assistance by foreign agencies makes local organizations reluctant to take relief measures; that relief efforts may obscure underlying political realities; that effective relief must see disaster assistance from the view of the victims and their requirements; that the reestablishment of the local economy is usually more important for disaster victims than material assistance.

It is clear that Fred Cuny was not just a practitioner; he was a perceptive student of emergencies. Most of his early ideas still ring true today, even when emergencies are much more complex, much more difficult to unravel. The lessons we take from Fred's written work live on. Many of Fred's ideas are at the center of a growing effort to question the traditional models of relief assistance and to refocus efforts on people's livelihoods, not just their survival. It is clearly not enough to save people's lives; we must also endeavor to save and bring back people's livelihoods.

Fred was clear that there were different approaches that could be taken in emergency relief. For him, the center of the effort had to be the victims, not the international relief agencies. Agencies that focused on fundraising, on raising their visibility, and on coming in with prepackaged programs were doing more harm than good. Fred laid out the options for agencies: respond in a traditional mode of relief that would be ineffective or respond in an innovative way that would accelerate recovery, fully cognizant of local politics and economics and relying heavily on local coping mechanisms and livelihood strategies.

In this primer, Fred takes these same ideas and focuses on famine. The world has changed since Fred wrote this book. But the underlying concepts of his book on famine, just like the underlying concepts in his work over twenty years ago, are valid. Fred had an ability to see the full picture, of placing disasters, emergencies, and famine within a broader perspective. He also trusted common people, poor people, to come up with solutions and ideas to help their recovery. For Fred, emergencies were opportunities to help people—not just to survive and live, but to change the social, economic, and political context of their lives to allow them to break out of poverty and oppression.

The Feinstein International Famine Center of Tufts University and World Vision are honored to help publish this primer on famine written by Fred Cuny. We knew Fred as a person and as a thinker; as a practitioner and as a student; as an innovator and creator; and as a listener who could translate experiences into lessons learned. We know that the lessons learned that are reflected in this book will be extremely useful to practitioners and students of famine and emergency response.

1 | *Famine and Its Causes*

Introduction

Famines are one of the scourges of mankind. They can kill large numbers of people, especially women and children, as well as spread disease and malnutrition. They can impoverish whole populations and dislocate families, villages, and entire societies. Finally, they can create or extend political instability. Famines and the conflicts that often establish and spread them leave wounds in a society that may take generations to heal.

There are two types of famines: those that result from a lack of food and those that happen because people lack purchasing power. Lack of purchasing power, an issue for the poor, is called an *entitlement problem*. Of the two, the lack of purchasing power is the most prevalent.

To combat famines, two approaches can be applied: *supplying food* and *providing economic support*. The relative effectiveness of each method is determined by when it is used. In most cases, food relief alone has a limited impact and is often counterproductive.

From these general approaches, two broad strategies for fighting famines have developed. The first, which revolves around food aid, can be called *conventional relief*. The second, which focuses on addressing the root causes of famine and is designed to prevent, contain, and control it with a range of economic and market interventions, can be called *counterfamine assistance*. If counterfamine measures are taken early, many famines can be prevented or quickly controlled.

Defining Famine

Famine may be defined *as a set of conditions that occur when large numbers of people in a region cannot obtain sufficient food, and widespread, acute malnutrition results*. Acute malnutrition occurs when people eat so little food that their body's store of nutrients is depleted. If the condition continues, people can die.

The primary consequence of famine is a significant increase in the number of deaths, or mortality, associated with inadequate food consumption. *Consumption levels*, not *food availability*, define a state of famine. Other consequences are a significant rise in rates of disease, or morbidity, and massive dislocation of populations.

Famine is an area-wide phenomenon. During famines, the local markets do not supply food at costs that a substantial number of the population can afford. Most people—including some who work in famine relief—believe famines occur when there is not enough food in an area to feed people. This is rarely true, even in conflict zones. Instead, famines occur when the poor do not have enough money to buy food when it is scarce and prices rise. Some amounts of food can usually be found even in countries in the midst of civil wars, including those with perpetual food deficits. In these countries, for example, people who live in urban areas can usually afford to buy higher-priced, imported foods. Only a few societies exist that cannot redistribute available food stocks to meet temporary needs—if they want to. That means famines are an economic and political problem more than a commodity deficit.

The best historical example of this is the Irish Potato Famine of 1851: at the height of the famine when poor Irishmen were starving, Ireland was exporting wheat and other grains to England at above-normal levels.

Famine and Chronic Nutritional Deficiencies

Many countries experience perpetual food shortages and distribution problems. These result in chronic and often widespread hunger among significant numbers of people. There is a difference, however, between famine and chronic malnutrition. Chronic malnutrition, or hunger, occurs when a large percentage of the population routinely lacks the financial resources to acquire sufficient food from available stocks or the types of food they can obtain are nutritionally deficient. In other words, they have a poor diet. Chronic hunger can be found in rich countries such as the United States as well as in poor nations such as India. Chronic hunger leads to stunted growth and physical deficiencies in individuals. Collectively, it leads to higher infant and child mortality but at rates far lower than in famines.

While chronic hunger is a major concern, approaches needed to eradicate it are different from those used to fight famine. Chronic hunger requires long-term institutional and developmental approaches.

Contemporary Famines

As recently as the 1970s, famines usually resulted from a combination of economic and environmental factors. However, after the great

Sahelian (African), Ethiopian, and Bangladeshi famines of that decade, the international community initiated a number of measures to increase food security at the international level. The international community made it easier to send food from the more productive counties to the third world and to increase food supplies in the most famine-prone countries. Significant strides were also made in developing systems to help warn of impending food shortages: satellites were able to detect drought conditions, and economic indicators were identified that gave reasonably accurate signals that food shortages were becoming critical.

As a result of these advances, famines should not be a significant threat. Nevertheless, they are. The reason: war and civil conflict. In almost every famine that occurred in the 1980s and 1990s, the country was at war, either with itself or with its neighbors. The Ethiopian famine of 1984–86 started in the war-torn provinces of Eritrea and Tigray. The Sudanese famine of the same period occurred as the civil war in the south assumed tragic proportions. And the Somali famine of 1991–92 was due almost entirely to factional fighting that disrupted the flow of food to people in all parts of the country.

A look at almost any famine today will find a country in conflict. In most cases, the famine will be in or adjacent to the war zone, but famine conditions may also develop in areas far from the fighting. In 1990, severe food shortages developed in western Sudan, largely because the government was spending all its efforts to fight the war in the south and was diverting food and transport to that area. When a drought occurred in the west, there was insufficient food to reallocate to the region. The rate for hiring trucks to move a small amount of food to the western part of the country made the market price prohibitively high for the poor. Furthermore, the government was unwilling to admit there was a problem. Government officials feared that, in an unstable political environment, admitting food problems existed would be seen as a failure of the administration or might further erode popular support for the war in the south.

Causes of Famine

Famines result from an unusual event or set of events striking a community where a significant number of people are already undernourished. They include:

- War, civil conflict, or social upheaval
- The failure of a harvest due to climatic or other environmental conditions such as drought, flood, wind, or insect infestation (primarily locusts)
- The disruption or collapse of the food-distribution network and/

or the marketing system, affecting a significant percentage of the population. Political, environmental, or economic crises could cause these events.

- Lack or disruption of an emergency food-support system that ensures the rural poor have access to food during shortages. This could include food banks, price supports, and transportation subsidies.

The two most common triggers for famines are conflict and drought.

War and Civil Conflict

Wars triggered most of the great famines of the late twentieth century. Examples of famine occurred during the Nigerian civil war (1968–70), the Bangladeshi civil war (1971), the armed insurrection in the northern Ethiopian provinces of Eritrea and Tigray (1984–85), widespread civil war in many parts of Mozambique after 1984, and the civil war in Somalia (1991–92). War not only contributes to the creation of famine, but it also disrupts famine-relief operations.

Conflict can trigger famine in a number of ways, including:

- Disrupting the agricultural cycle
- Driving farmers from the land
- Disrupting marketing processes
- Destroying stores of harvested foods
- Creating food shortages that drive prices above levels that low-income families can pay

Not every war creates famine conditions. In a number of cases, both government and rebel forces have ensured that food supplies were available throughout a conflict. During the long troubles in Lebanon, for example, no major food shortages occurred. In El Salvador and during the Nicaraguan civil war in the late 1970s, insurgent forces took steps to make sure food was provided to people in rebel-held areas. As a general rule, however, the chances that a rebel force can create alternative-distribution sources for people under its control decreases as the area of conflict gets larger and the potential supply line gets longer.

Throughout history, famine has been used as an instrument of war. In recent years, disturbing instances have occurred when some governments have tried to deny food to populations as a deliberate weapon to control rebel areas. However, a famine created or prolonged for military purposes is an ultimately ineffective tool. Such famine is indiscriminate and attacks only people who are least likely to be combatants: children, pregnant and nursing women, and the elderly. They die first and in the largest numbers.

Proponents of total war argue that famines undermine the morale of fighters, increasing desertion and weakening their will to fight. However, there is no evidence to support this contention. In fact, waging war against civilians usually solidifies support for the resident combatants. The Nigerians used starvation as a weapon against Biafra, but the region held out despite almost 1.5 million deaths—mainly women and children. The rebel army never ran out of food and resisted until its last small enclave was defeated (Mayer 1981). The point is: combatants always receive priority for food—those with guns rarely starve.

Drought

A drought is any unusual, prolonged dry period. While droughts are usually associated with semiarid or desert climates, they can occur in areas that usually have adequate rainfall. Technically, a drought is a condition of climatic dryness severe enough to reduce soil moisture and water supplies below the minimums necessary for sustaining plant, animal, and human life. They are often accompanied by dry, hot winds and may be terminated by violent storms.

The consequences of drought can be divided according to the primary, or immediate, effects and the secondary, or resulting, ones.

Drought occurs when there is an extended reduction of water available for agricultural pursuit. As a dry period progresses, existing water supplies are overtaxed and eventually dry up. Crops, livestock, and other animals are lost. Finally, there is no water for washing, bathing, or drinking.

Drought also has secondary results. As water supplies dwindle and crops and fodder are depleted, families leave their homes to look for better grazing lands for their remaining livestock. Some of the families may migrate to cities, seeking jobs or alternative sources of income. If dwindling food supplies are not replaced, famine can occur, accelerating migration. The migration may contribute to the spread of the disaster, especially if grazing animals are moved with the people.

If the drought is long term, it may result in permanent changes in settlement, social, and living patterns. For example, before the 1968 drought in Mauritania, 65 percent of the people were nomads. By 1976, that figure had dropped to 36 percent. The town of Nouakchott, the country's capital, grew from 12,300 in 1964 to approximately 135,000 ten years later.

Complex Famines

Multiple factors—usually war and drought—trigger complex famines. Such situations complicate relief operations. Complex famines usually

Figure 1-1

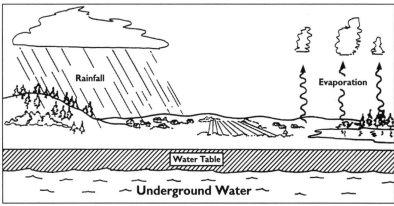

NORMAL HYDROLOGICAL BALANCE: Water supply is adequate to meet demand. The community grows and land use intensifies.

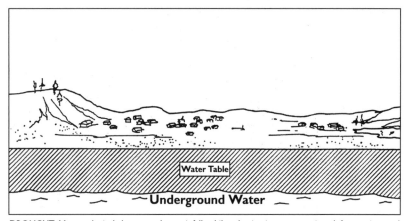

DROUGHT: Meteorological changes reduce rainfall, while urbanization, overgrazing, deforestation, and farming reduce the soil's water retention. The normal hydrological balance is broken. The topsoil erodes and the water table is lowered, making recovery difficult. Food production and drinking water are reduced, and people migrate out of the area.

occur in Africa. Recent examples include northern Ethiopia (1977–78 and 1984–85), Mozambique (1984–88), and Somalia (1991–92).

Famine Vulnerability

Societies vulnerable to famine have several characteristics: residents are often subsistence farmers or pastoralists (people dependent on livestock), they are poor and underemployed, the number of landless people is high, and the debt of both individuals and the country is great.

Famine usually occurs in rural areas and rarely spreads to urban zones, except when the displaced move there. People who produce food are the ones most likely to starve. Why are poor farmers and herdsmen so vulnerable? Farmers face continual risks from the time they plant their seeds until they harvest their crops and sell them. Figure 1–2 shows those factors. If problems occur, the harvest could range from marginal to total failure.

Subsistence agriculture has the following characteristics:

- Farmers' plots are small and often fragmented

- Tools and implements are primitive

- Farmers gear production to feeding their families, not to selling crops

- Few alternative or seasonal employment opportunities exist

- People have little surplus grain or cash reserves

Subsistence farmers rarely grow only one crop—even though their land might produce more that way. Instead, families attempt to grow almost all their needs for the entire year. Often, however, they fail to achieve their objective, their produce lasting only six to nine months. For the vast majority of peasants, output is so low that they cannot establish grain reserves. At the village and regional level, subsistence-farming communities rarely have food reserves available. Whole regions are perpetually vulnerable to famine if there is no means for releasing food into those areas when famine conditions occur.

Figure 1-2

Linear Diagram of Subsistence Farming

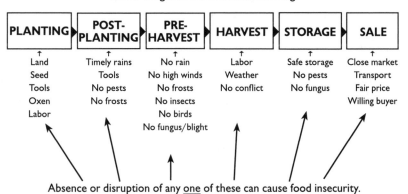

Absence or disruption of any <u>one</u> of these can cause food insecurity.

Subsistence agriculture often produces the kind of food that makes it difficult for the human body to survive famines. Many food-scarce societies depend on cassava, maize, and other carbohydrate-rich, protein-poor foods. These foods provide necessary calories, but in mono-diet regions, where only one kind of carbohydrate-rich food is consumed, food-nutrient deficiencies disable the body's ability to function properly. Societies that depend on such foods are nutritionally vulnerable from the outset. Without sufficient amounts of essential nutrients, the body's ability to efficiently metabolize food is reduced, and it begins to starve, even when food amounts are minimally adequate.

Subsistence farmers usually have two ways of ensuring they will have enough food: growing grain and raising livestock. When a harvest fails, they trade their livestock for grain. The price of sheep and goats varies from culture to culture. However, when grain prices increase, more animals have to be sold to obtain the same amount of grain. As more and more animals are sold, the market becomes saturated, and the value of livestock declines. When the number of animals per sack of grain doubles, it usually triggers panic sales of livestock, decreasing their price even more. When people can no longer afford a whole sack of grain, they buy in smaller quantities. Merchants then increase prices to sustain their income on a lower volume of sales.

The livestock market may collapse, and grain prices throughout the affected region may increase. Ultimately, it may take ten small animals to buy one sack of grain. When that happens, the purchasing power of subsistence farmers is ravaged, since few are likely to have had more than a couple dozen goats or sheep to begin with and some of those may have been lost to drought or conflict. (A bag of grain usually contains forty or fifty kilos, depending on the type of grain involved. Since an average person eats 300 grams per day, a bag of grain will provide between 200 and 250 person days of grain.)

Pastoralists are also vulnerable to famine. Few nomads, for example, raise animals to eat—animals are a trading commodity, and pastoralists exchange them for grain and other foods. When the livestock market collapses, they have few other resources for food.

Environmental Factors

Frequent crop failures in Ethiopia, Somalia, and the Sahel have been attributed in recent years, at least in part, to progressive deterioration of the land. Deforestation, poor agricultural practices, and overgrazing have produced rapid desertification and extensive soil erosion.

As vegetation is stripped from the land, the surface dries out and reflects more of the sun's heat. This can alter the thermal dynamics of the atmosphere and suppress rainfall. More land then dries out. Removing grasses by overgrazing or slash-and-burn agriculture also erodes the land, and cutting trees increases the rate of wind and water erosion, especially in hilly areas.

Poverty and Famine Vulnerability

The poor suffer most in a famine; they are vulnerable, because they are poor (Cuny 1994). Recognizing poverty as the root of vulnerability to famine is the first step in creating a more rational and developmental approach to famine assistance.

Those aspects of poverty that contribute to famine vulnerability include unjust land-tenure patterns; inequitable farming practices, especially sharecropping; tribal or racial discrimination that prevents adequate resources from reaching large groups of subsistence farmers; exploitative merchants and land owners who keep the poor under control by making sure they remain in debt; and production practices such as cheap labor and lower costs for big suppliers that hold the poor in marginal circumstances.

There is also a relation between poverty, family size, and famine vulnerability. Poorly paid workers tend to have large families, since more workers are needed for the family to survive. However, children rarely earn enough to pay their cost of living, so the earnings of the adults must support more people, leading to a smaller per capita income. When that income is tied to subsistence agriculture, shortfalls affect more people.

The Most Affected Groups

The three groups hardest hit by famines are the families of subsistence farmers, pastoralists, and displaced people who have moved to urban areas. Among poor families, the ones most at risk are children between nine months and five years, women, pregnant and lactating mothers, and the elderly. Deaths and illness affect these groups first, so their health and nutritional status is considered a reliable indicator and an early warning of problems affecting the overall population. These groups are the most vulnerable, because:

- Their nutrition needs are higher
- They are less able to provide for themselves: young children depend on their mothers for survival, and women with dependent children often have a difficult time leaving home to work
- Parents often must make cruel decisions concerning who will get enough food to live and who will die. In these cases, working-age males are usually the most likely to receive food. Children who have reached five years—when their chances of survival

are statistically greater and they can begin to earn income or share in routine family chores—tend to receive preference over younger children (Mayer 1981). Some family members must be sacrificed sometimes if others are to live. The first to be abandoned may be the elderly or the infirm, then gradually and subconsciously, infant children are factored out of the family's food distribution.

- Among children, the most vulnerable are those who have been recently weaned, because another child has been born who must be nursed. In many parts of the developing world, especially Africa, children at this age receive little protein-rich food, even when it is available. Protein is saved for people who work.

Visitors to famine areas often do not see many people in the risk groups; they usually are secluded, especially if they are weak or ill. Visible absence of these groups is due to both cultural and practical factors. Those who are exceptionally ill are usually in a dwelling or tent. They do not join the crowds attracted by outside visitors, and they don't participate in distributions of food, because they are too weak. Cultural requirements sometimes insist that women, particularly if they are pregnant, nursing, or have recently given birth, avoid being seen by outsiders, especially men.

Political Aspects of Vulnerability

Amartya Sen, a renowned famine researcher, has written: "There is no such thing as an apolitical food problem" (1981). The distribution of food within a country is a political issue. Governments in most countries give priority to urban areas, since that is where the most influential and powerful families and enterprises are usually located. The government often neglects subsistence farmers and rural areas in general. The more remote and underdeveloped the area, the less likely the government will be to effectively meet its needs. If people in the area have any political differences with the government, neglect may be intentional.

Many agrarian policies, especially the pricing of agricultural commodities, discriminate against rural areas. Governments often keep prices for basic grains at such artificially low levels that subsistence producers cannot accumulate enough capital to make investments to improve their production. Thus, they are effectively prevented from getting out of their precarious situation. Comprehensive agricultural policies and commodity pricing standards that permit subsistence farmers to accumulate capital must be developed if an effective strategy to counter famine is to be created.

Famine is often the result of drastic political or economic changes brought on when governments adopt new policies or economic systems. An extreme example of such a change occurred in Cambodia in the 1970s, when several million people may have died, because the Khmer Rouge government harshly enforced its vision of a new society. Another example happened in China from 1958 to 1962 during the Great Leap Forward, when political policies took farmers away from food production, creating a famine that killed an estimated thirty million people, far more than anyone imagined at the time.

Militias in Somalia during the conflict/famine there stole the international community's relief assistance, compelling humanitarian agencies to continue sending in food and other assistance. Then the warlords confiscated that food as well. However, less dramatic political or economic changes can also lead to famine conditions. These changes can include:

- New land-use policies
- Villagization. The formation of villages to provide infrastructure and services is often the forerunner of forced collectivization of agricultural land.
- Collectivization
- Forced relocation/resettlement
- Changes in agricultural-commodity price structures
- Changes in cropping patterns
- Changes in the cost of such agricultural items as seeds and tools

Economic Factors

Markets can create or contribute to famine conditions. A situation called *demand failure* develops when the poor do not have enough money to buy available food. In other words, there is no demand. Merchants then move food stocks to areas where people do have money. A second problem occurs when the market cannot provide enough food, even though people have money to buy it. This is known as *supply failure*.

The extent to which regional food shortages are translated into regional food-price rises depends on the degree that markets are integrated (Devereux and Hay 1986). In an integrated market, supply and demand can be coordinated. When the two are not coordinated, one has a *fragmented market*. Fragmented markets can occur, for example, when food cannot be moved, because guerrillas control the countryside, restricting the government to urban areas. Dramatic rises in local food prices, which reflect market fragmentation, are symptomatic of food shortages.

If markets are integrated and function reasonably well according to supply and demand, regional food shortages rarely lead to famine, since shortfalls of supplies can be replaced from other markets with little effect on prices or consumption in the affected regions.

As Frances Stewart has pointed out, lags in price adjustment can also cause famines. For example, if prices rise dramatically and agricultural wages do not follow immediately, low-income people starve. These critical time lags would not cause starvation if people had savings or access to loans. But because they are poor, they lack these things. This is another illustration of how poverty and famine vulnerability are related (Stewart 1982).

Rising inflation and/or rising unemployment leave the poor with little or no money to buy goods and may lead to the collapse of the market system. In these cases, the government must act quickly to ensure food can be distributed from relief sources on an equitable basis. Otherwise, imagined scarcity, hoarding, and price manipulation may fuel the onset of famine conditions.

Transportation

Inadequate transportation systems or disruption of transport often influence price increases during food crises. Rural areas need cheap and constant access to transport, especially lorries (trucks), to ship food out when prices are favorable and to import food at reasonable prices when shortages exist. In the Tigray area of Ethiopia, for example, transportation costs accounted for two-thirds of the price of food during shortages in 1990. The disruption of transportation systems is more significant during conflicts than in normal times.

A General Famine Model

In 1985, Peter Cutler of the Relief and Development Institute produced a model (Figure 1–3) that approximates the sequence of events leading to a major famine. The model, however, does not account for war—though many of the disruptions shown could occur as a result of conflict. It also gives little indication of the timing of these events. For example, in Asia, which has a high percentage and density of landless peasants, the sequence could occur in several months. In Africa, however, people tend to have larger herds of livestock they can sell, and they traditionally migrate in search of alternative work when food shortages or conflicts occur. Therefore, it may take several years of poor harvests or war before famine conditions are established.

This model is a general one and cannot be applied to every country. However, detailed studies in famine-prone regions, especially from the viewpoint of the small farmer, can lead to the development of models for specific areas that could help forecast famines and pinpoint counterfamine interventions.

Figure 1-3

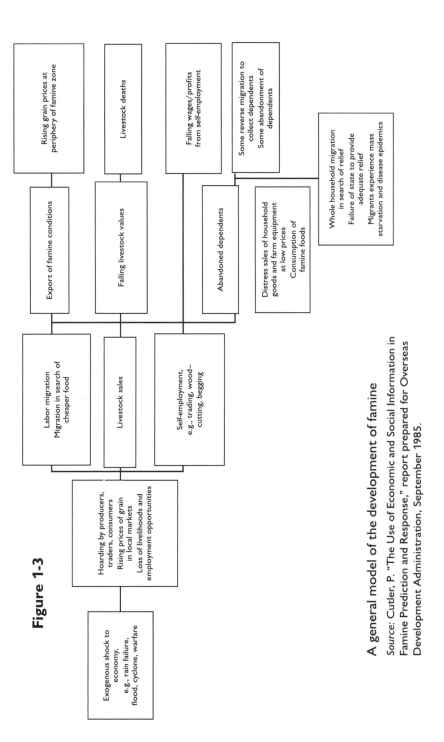

A general model of the development of famine

Source: Cutler, P. "The Use of Economic and Social Information in Famine Prediction and Response," report prepared for Overseas Development Administration, September 1985.

Figure 1-4

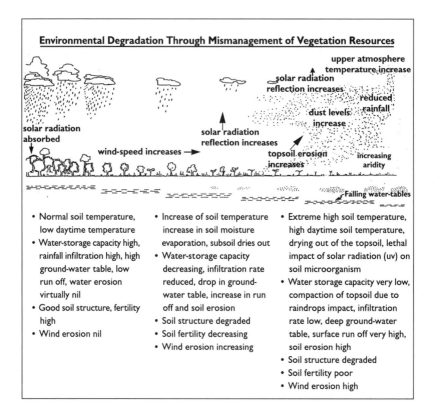

Environmental Degradation Through Mismanagement of Vegetation Resources

- Normal soil temperature, low daytime temperature
- Water-storage capacity high, rainfall infiltration high, high ground-water table, low run off, water erosion virtually nil
- Good soil structure, fertility high
- Wind erosion nil

- Increase of soil temperature increase in soil moisture evaporation, subsoil dries out
- Water-storage capacity decreasing, infiltration rate reduced, drop in ground-water table, increase in run off and soil erosion
- Soil structure degraded
- Soil fertility decreasing
- Wind erosion increasing

- Extreme high soil temperature, high daytime soil temperature, drying out of the topsoil, lethal impact of solar radiation (uv) on soil microorganism
- Water storage capacity very low, compaction of topsoil due to raindrops impact, infiltration rate low, deep ground-water table, surface run off very high, soil erosion high
- Soil structure degraded
- Soil fertility poor
- Wind erosion high

Famine Phases

Cutler's model can be divided into three phases based on the types of coping strategies people use. During the first phase, families remain at home and sell assets such as livestock to buy grain. During the second period, they sell critical assets such as tools and draught animals and may send some family members out of the community to seek work. In the third phase, whole families migrate in search of work or food.

For emergency-relief managers, these phases provide a key for planning counterfamine and relief strategies. As long as families remain intact, the famine is in the developing stages, and relief agencies should focus their efforts on providing opportunities for families to earn cash to increase their economic security. The second phase marks the borderline between hunger and disaster—economic interventions should continue, but some forms of food aid will be required. The third phase is a full-scale emergency. Lifesaving interventions focusing on food and nutrition, public health, and disease control predominate. While economic assistance is still possible, and indeed vital, agencies will be so involved in emergency food aid that few will have the time, resources, or inclination to tackle wider problems.

Causes and Effects of Drought

Human activities contribute to the development of droughts. Overgrazing, poor cropping methods, and improper soil-conservation techniques often help create droughts. Drought feeds upon itself: vegetation is stripped from the land, and the surface dries out and reflects more of the sun's heat. This alters the thermal dynamics of the atmosphere and suppresses rainfall, which in turn dries out more land. (See Figure 1–4.)

The effects of drought can be divided according to the primary, or immediate, effects and the secondary, or resulting, effects.

Lack of water produces the primary effects of a drought. As a dry period progresses, existing water supplies are overtaxed and eventually dry up. Crops, livestock, and other animals are lost. Finally, there is no water for washing, bathing, or drinking.

The secondary effects of drought follow. As water supplies dwindle and crops and fodder are depleted, families leave their homes to look for better grazing lands for their herds. Some of the families may migrate to the cities, seeking jobs or alternative sources of income. If dwindling food supplies are not replaced, famine can occur, accelerating migration. This migration may contribute to the spread of the disaster, especially if grazing animals are moved with the people.

If the drought is long term, it may result in permanent changes in settlement patterns and in social and living arrangements. For example, before the 1968 drought in Mauritania, 65 percent of the people were nomads. By 1976, that figure had dropped to 36 percent. The Mauritanian capital, Nouakchott, grew from 12,300 in 1964 to approximately 135,000 ten years later.

Other secondary effects of drought include major ecological changes: increased desertification, scrub growth, the possibility of flash flooding, and wind erosion of soils. Of these problems, desertification is the most serious. Technically, desertification occurs when soil reaches a certain level of dryness and the land takes on characteristics of a desert. In its most dramatic form, sand dunes encroach, and most of the vegetation dies or is replaced by scrub brushes and other desert plants. The land becomes useless without large-scale and expensive reclamation measures.

People's Definitions of Famine

Most definitions of famine come from social scientists or relief workers. These definitions are often different from those used by people affected by famine. Two examples:

From Sudan: The people of Darfur often divide famines into *maja'a,* an ordinary famine, and *maja'al katale,* famines that kill. Ordinary famines might be better translated as periods of want or dearth, when people are forced to do unpleasant things to survive. Famines that kill are equated with starvation (de Waal 1988).

From Bangladesh: The culture defines three types of famine: scarcity is *akal* (when times are bad) and *durvickha* (when alms are scarce). Nationwide famine is *mananthor* (when the epoch changes) (Currey 1981).

2 | *Consequences of Famine*

The consequences of famine go far beyond acute malnutrition: large numbers of people die.

Famines increase the risk of disease. As the human body deteriorates, it becomes more susceptible to disease and vitamin deficiencies. Measles, cholera, diarrhea, tuberculosis, and xerophthalmia (Vitamin A deficiency) are of special concern.

In addition, famines create economic hardship for the rural poor. They can lose cash, livestock, and the assets needed for future production such as seeds, draught animals, and breeding livestock. As conditions persist, an economic regression may occur for the entire community or region.

At some point, people may leave their land to search for food. This can lead to mass migrations within a country, and in conflicts, it can cause migration from one country to another. For example, in 1984–85, Ethiopia witnessed both phenomena. Large numbers of people migrated to relief centers within the country, while several hundred thousand residents of the provinces of Tigray and Eritrea crossed the border into Sudan, seeking food.

These effects, if left unchecked, can set the stage for the next famine. In other words, if corrective measures are not taken, vulnerability to famine will probably increase.

Effect on the Human Body

During the history of humankind, food shortages have been frequent, and the human body has developed the capacity for resisting such them.

Under normal conditions and for short periods, the human body can get by on a minimum of 400 to 600 calories (usually described as kcals) of energy daily. The World Food Programme (WFP) of the United Nations and the United Nations High Commissioner for Refugees

(UNHCR) have set 1,900 kcals as the amount the average person needs each day. As food deprivation occurs, the body tries to maintain an adequate supply of energy in the brain and central nervous system by taking protein from tissues and fat reserves in the body.

Death from starvation occurs when about one-third of the body weight has been lost. Weight loss of a lesser degree can result in disturbances of the body's water balance, leading to famine edema (an abnormal accumulation of fluid in the body) and diarrhea caused by atrophy and ulceration of the intestines (Den Hartog 1981).

Carbohydrate-rich, protein-poor food, which is the mainstay of the diet in many subsistence societies, can complicate the nutritional situation for famine victims and is an important consideration when providing food relief. This, combined with the inadequacy of protein in available food, may lead to severe physiological imbalance and to protein-deficiency malnutrition. Young children, whose normal protein demands are high, are susceptible to this pattern (Cox 1981). In older children and adults, the effects of protein deficiency may be reversible to some extent, but such deficiency in infancy may lead to irreversible brain damage. Starvation also affects several mechanisms of disease resistance, reducing the body's capacity to produce antibodies and its ability to heal wounds.

Disease

Disease often accompanies famine. Infectious diseases are more likely to be transmitted during famines because of unusual population movements and the increased susceptibility of people to disease. The effects of diseases are more severe when they attack malnourished people. In addition, unclean water and food and poor sanitation can compound the situation. As people move in search of food, sanitary conditions in the camps and temporary settlements deteriorate quickly.

In general, the diseases that become epidemic during famines are already present in the population. The most serious infectious disease is measles.

Famine and Endemic Disease

Famine affects the susceptibility of individuals to a particular disease by changing the epidemiological characteristics of a community. The more social disruption occurs, the more disease there is. Epidemic disease develops when both individual and community resistance to infectious disease is lost. As people who have been searching for food are crowded into camps where sanitation is poor, each person is exposed to increasingly large doses of infectious agents. Some infectious diseases that are endemic (commonly found) in an area may not cause significant disease, because most people have already been exposed to them and have acquired a degree of natural immunization. However, some endemic diseases are poor natural immunizers, such as bacillary dysentery, and they can become major causes of death.

Measles is an acute viral disease of children, normally lethal only to children under five years of age. However, it the scourge of malnourished populations, and it killed as many as 50 percent of the Ethiopian children who died in refugee camps in Sudan during the famine of 1984–85 (Toole et al 1989). However, the severity of measles may vary depending on the type of malnutrition—calorie or protein deficiency—that the population is experiencing. For example, studies of measles in the refugee camps of East Bengal, India, in 1971 and in the Bangladeshi camps during the 1974 famine indicated only a small percentage of children in those communities died from the disease, leading many medical personnel to conclude that measles is less a threat in Asia than on other continents. Nonetheless, immunization against measles should always be carried out as a precaution, especially in Africa, where the disease among the malnourished is often fatal.

Preventive measures against diseases must also be considered within the context of each region. Antimalarial medicines are important only if malaria is not common in the area where people originated but prevalent in the area where they are taking temporary refuge. This is especially important when nonimmunized populations migrate to hyperendemic areas, or regions where high rates of the disease are found. Supplementing food rations with Vitamins A and C are essential in most countries where the population subsists largely on grain.

Other concerns are tuberculosis and various louse-borne diseases such as typhus, since their transmission is increased in overcrowded areas.

Diarrheal Diseases

Diarrheal diseases, primarily bacillary dysentery, quickly become widespread in famine. Dysentery or severe diarrhea is readily recognized by a bloody stool. Natural immunization of the intestinal tract is usually inadequate to protect the person, so one attack is quickly followed by another.

Diarrheal disease has been common in famines for a long time. Effective controls for dysentery are clean water, sanitation, and improved personal-hygiene practices. Oral rehydration therapy (ORT) will effectively reduce the number of deaths from diarrhea. Unfortunately, sanitation and good hygiene are usually the first casualties in a starving community or in a famine camp.

The key fact to remember is this: diarrhea kills through dehydration. Although a great array of bacteria, viruses, and parasites can cause diarrhea, it is usually the loss of water and salt from the body that brings about death. That means diarrhea therapy does not require laborious and costly lab searches for the pathogens. Nor are drugs necessary. Normal body mechanisms will fight off the pathogens within two to five days. And in any case, there is no known drug treatment for most diarrheal pathogens.

In the past, fluid replacement was considered a clinical problem. Intravenous infusions in expensive rehydration units saved the majority of the few who were within reach of such treatment. However, the same results can be accomplished using a mixture of ordinary sugar, salt, water, potassium chloride, and soda, which cost only a few cents, and can be administered orally. (See Chapter 9.)

Disease control in times of famine must compete with overwhelming needs for food, water, and shelter. Thus, measures must be inexpensive, culturally acceptable, highly effective, and easy to administer.

Psychological Changes

Psychological changes may occur in famines along with physiological changes. The unusual conditions that exist during famines cause many unusual patterns of behavior.

People in areas affected by famine are often depressed and apathetic. In densely populated or confined situations, such as those in displaced-persons or refugee camps, these changes often compound the relief problem.

Starvation conditions direct people's thoughts and activities toward food; most other activities are inhibited. Food-seeking activities are sometimes directed toward the principal staple that the population has normally depended on, often at the expense of other potential sources. Usually, however, the range of foods sought and eaten is broadened to include many foods not normally considered edible. Ultimately, breeding livestock and seed grain may be consumed, compounding future food-supply problems.

Social Impact

Impact on Family Units

When family members are forced to leave home in search of food, their ties with home, farm, and even some family members are weakened. Eventually wandering bands of individuals seeking food begin to appear.

When family members are sent to find food, some families may lose their breadwinners. Thus, relief workers often find a large percentage of families headed by women.

Mass migration is a major sign that famine conditions are developing. A famine is not usually over until a majority of those who left have been returned or are permanently resettled.

Impact on the Community

As famines progress, normal social behavior is increasingly affected. Initially, there will be mutual help between family members or families,

---

The Madras Famine of 1876–78

A surgeon in the British Indian army carried out one of the first systematic studies that linked famine and disease during the Madras famine of 1876–78. The doctor, Alexander Porter, studied the diseases that occurred in the relief camps attached to the hospital where he worked. He used his spare time to perform 459 autopsies on those who died of starvation and its complications. The study remains useful and thought provoking a century later.

The trouble in Madras began in 1875 after the southwest monsoon failed for two consecutive years. Famine conditions developed in a large area containing a population of 1.4 million. Merchants and speculators who were hoarding food exacerbated this natural calamity. Prices rose far beyond what poor people could pay. Famine followed.

Porter noted that diarrhea and dysentery were the most prevalent of the many diseases that occurred in the relief camps. Within the sheds where Porter worked, 34 percent of the patients who were admitted died. Dysentery and diarrhea were responsible for 77 percent of the deaths and were equally important in adults and children.

Porter published his findings in 1889, establishing a link between famine and dysentery and showing the illness was one of the principal causes of death. It still provides us with one of the major keys to understanding the interventions required.

Source: J. R. K. Robson, editor, *Famine: Its Causes, Effects and Management* (New York: Gordon & Breach Science Publishers, 1981), 62.

but in a later stage, people may care only for themselves. In the worst cases, social cohesion begins to fail. Traditional leaders who are unable to effectively redistribute food in the community may find their leadership challenged or ignored.

Food distribution may cause serious social and economic side effects. Such distribution is often handled in a way that circumvents traditional local leaders. When this occurs, it threatens to destroy traditional leadership and can affect the bonds of society. Too much free food over a long period can be a disincentive to people to return to work, especially agricultural production. Numerous writers have pointed out the danger of creating relief dependency (Jackson and Eade 1982).

Table 2-A

SERIOUSNESS OF DYSENTERY IN FAMINES

Dysentery was one of the two largest causes of death during the Bangladesh famine of 1974.

Causes of death by sex and disease in Dacca between October 1974 and January 1975 (percentages are for all diseases) are shown in the following table.

Cause	Male	Female	Total	Percent
Dysentery	335	393	728	36.0
Diarrhea	4	7	11	0.5
Malnutrition	172	142	314	15.0
Measles	–	2	2	0.1
Exposure	14	8	22	1.1
Fever	369	466	835	41.0
Smallpox	–	1	1	0.1
Other Infectious Neurological Diseases	16	19	35	1.7
Others	51	31	82	4.3
TOTAL	961	1,069	2,030	

Source: Rahaman, M. "The Causes and Effects of Famine in the Rural Population: A Report from Bangladesh," in J.R.K. Robson, editor, *Famine: Its Causes, Effects and Management* (New York: Gordon & Breach Science Publishers, 1981), 138.

3 | *Geography of Famine*

Geographic Distribution of Famines

While famines can occur anywhere there is a war, they are most likely to develop in areas that have long dry periods each year followed by short rainy seasons, possibly only a couple of months long. If the rains are delayed or do not come, farmers can lose everything they have planted. Subsistence farmers do not have adequate resources to outlast frequent failures.

Two *famine belts* exist in the world. The first extends from Europe into Central Asia and on into northern China. Food-production failures can occur in this region, because it is damp and cold and has shortened growing seasons. The second runs from Africa around the Mediterranean eastward through the dry and monsoon lands of southern Asia to China. In this belt, droughts may trigger famines, although war is the primary cause today.

The modernization of Europe, the former Soviet Union, and, more recently, China has almost eliminated the threat of natural famine in the northern belt. A notable exception, however, was the severe famine in China during the Great Leap Forward, mentioned in Chapter 1. However, crop failures in those regions can affect the availability of food in other parts of the world. The Soviet Union's large grain purchases in the 1970s, for example, drove the worldwide price of food so high that many food-short countries began exporting food, a situation that led to famine conditions in large areas of Sahelian Africa.

When crops do fail, governments provide assistance, sometimes buying food in massive quantities on the world market. These assistance programs—aided by good transportation systems—buffer the year-to-year variability in food production and prevent local crop failures from causing local famine.

This kind of development, however, has not occurred as extensively in the African and Asian drought belt. Transportation and communication in some areas are so poor that famine conditions may go unrecognized. Even when they become known, the mechanics of distributing aid during conflicts over large areas with primitive road networks can prove almost insurmountable.

There is nothing in North or South America comparable to the famine belt of Africa and Asia. Nevertheless, some regions are arid environments or have variable year-to-year rainfalls, most notably northeastern Brazil. The apparent absence of famines in North and South America, however, may be the result of poor record keeping and the failure of governments to recognize when famine conditions exist. But, more importantly, highly marginal subsistence agriculture prevails throughout most of Latin America and the Caribbean. The failure of these countries to diversify their agricultural systems—coupled with high unemployment and political unrest—leave them vulnerable to famines. An outbreak of violence or a natural disaster could trigger widespread food shortages.

Another concern in the Americas is environmental degradation. As it becomes more widespread, the risk of famine will increase in many countries. For example, massive deforestation in Haiti—and the resulting loss of topsoil—has placed that country at the top of the list of places in the Western Hemisphere with a high potential for famine. During the political turmoil there in 1993–95, large infusions of food aid were required to prevent severe malnutrition.

A 1984 study of displaced people in El Salvador showed pockets of high malnutrition and infant mortality that, in other circumstances, would indicate famine or near-famine conditions. A study of one San Salvador barrio revealed a higher annual death rate than that experienced in Biafra in 1969 at the height of the Nigerian civil war (Bureau for Refugee Programs 1984).

Famine Shift

One of the most important things to understand about famine is how it shifts inside a country or region. One region may be recovering while another is declining. Grasping how and why famines move can provide planners with insight on how to use their resources to counter and prevent the spread of famine.

Why do famines shift? Shifting occurs when food from areas of marginal production is drawn into areas of severe shortage, because prices are higher. The movement of food out of an area causes prices to rise there, making it difficult for poor people to buy food. When this happens, the nutritional status of people in the marginal areas begins to decline.

Ethiopia is an example. The Ethiopian geographer Mesfin Wolde-

Mariam, who has mapped famines in Ethiopia dating back to the late 1800s, says famines move in a "tightening circle" around the country. Ethiopia is perpetually in famine, he points out. The conditions simply shift from region to region. Wolde-Mariam illustrates the effect of this phenomenon, which he calls *spatial extension*, in Figure 3–1 (Wolde-Mariam 1981).

The importance of famine shift becomes clear when the number of *awrajas* (subdistricts) in Ethiopia that experience famine conditions is examined. In a twenty-year period (1958–77) examined by Wolde-Mariam, only seven *awrajas* out of 102 in the country did not have famine. In 1958, twelve *awrajas* experienced famine, and in most of the subsequent nineteen years, one or more new *awrajas* had famines. In fact, on average, four new *awrajas* each year had famines. Only three years—1967, 1968, and 1971—saw no new areas with famine. By the end of 1966, eighty-one of the country's 102 *awrajas* had experienced famine. This means that in the following twelve years, famine conditions revisited areas that had already had famines in the previous decade (Wolde-Mariam 1981).

The larger the contiguous area experiencing famine, the greater the destructive capacity and the greater the likelihood that the conditions that fuel the famine will become perpetual.

Relief Management

Understanding how famines shift is the first step in developing a famine containment strategy. Such an understanding points to areas that require immediate aid as well as those that will next need attention. Understanding famine shift can help relief planners determine which areas need to be monitored and assessed. It can also provide guidance for the types of assistance needed in different regions. For example, a good strategy to use at the edge of a famine zone is increasing the amount of food available to the poor through food-for-work or cash-for-work programs (see Chapter 8). Relief officials failed to increase the availability of food in markets outside the original famine zone in Ethiopia after the 1984–85 famine, which contributed to the continuation of major food shortages for the poor in adjoining areas in 1987–88.

Figure 3-1

Spatial Extension of Famine

L=local   R=regional   N=national

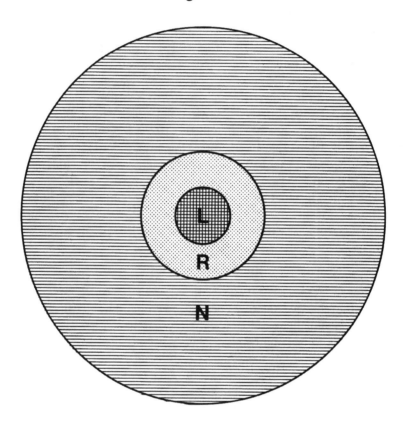

All other things remaining equal,
potential supply area for L is R + N.
potential supply area for R is N.
potential supply area for N is external.

As the famine area expands,
the potential demand increases,
while the potential supply area diminishes.

4 | *Societal Responses to Famine*

Introduction

Communities with frequent food shortages often develop family and community mechanisms for coping with famine. It is vital to understand these strategies. They are a factor in supplying the amount of food available in a famine zone. They can also indicate what stage a famine is in. Famine relief should be provided in such a way that the traditional means of coping are not disrupted.

Pastoralists and subsistence farmers store excess production from a good season to meet food needs during a bad one. For pastoral or semipastoral peoples, this storage is usually in natural form: their animals, the grasses and other forage on range lands, the supplementary plant and animal foods collected, and the fat reserves on their own bodies.

In subsistence-crop production, some food is stored in artificial form, such as silos and bins. Some foods may be dried while others are buried (Cox 1981).

Agricultural Adjustments

The subsistence-food-production systems of people in famine zones show many adaptations. The diversified and mobile systems of pastoralism practiced in Africa, the Middle East, and Central Asia provide clear examples. In the Cunene and Cuanhama regions of Angola, for example, pastoral people practice a combination of cattle herding, farming, gathering, and fishing activities. Herds are moved seasonally in response to range conditions. The Karamajong people of northeastern Uganda show a similar pattern: women cultivate sorghum, maize, and millet near permanent villages, while men and boys herd cattle, sheep, and goats. Diversification has advantages. People do not depend completely on crops, which could fail in any given year because of inadequate rainfall, or on animal herds, which could be destroyed by disease or poor range conditions.

Similar arguments may be made for many subsistence systems of farming. Mixed cropping—planting several crops together—is common in areas where rainfall is seasonal. Such practices maximize both production and economic benefit while minimizing the risk of complete crop failure.

Table 4–A shows the responses of farmers interviewed in Tanzania in 1971 that indicated they practiced a wide variety of adjustments during drought situations. The survey showed that famine-threatened communities often have attempted to adjust their agricultural and animal-husbandry patterns by planting reserve famine crops and resowing cereals and other food plants. These actions may be repeated many times before they are abandoned. Alternatively, people may decide to search for more suitable agricultural lands and pastures.

Survival Strategies of Subsistence Farmers

Most subsistence farmers try to ensure they have enough grain for their households before they plant cash crops. And they try to plant sufficient grain to feed their families even if the rains are poor. If the rains are good, they can store or sell the extra grain. Some grains can be stored safely for several years in any one of several storage methods used in traditional societies, such as burying it in sealed jars. Households can also invest in animals, which can be sold in times of hardship. Others will trade their excess grain for cash or gold and hide it.

Planting decisions also show the farmers' concern for food security. Where possible, they plant drought-resistant strains of grain. If land is readily available, farmers may plant larger areas than they can maintain; only those fields receiving adequate rainfall will be weeded and cultivated. In some societies, farmers may have widely dispersed fields. That way, they can take advantage of scattered rainfalls (de Waal 1988).

Adjustments by Pastoralists

Pastoralists usually use a variety of risk-reduction strategies. Herders, who are faced with the double threats of drought and disease, are more vulnerable to famine than farmers. They do not grow food staples. Instead, they usually buy them in the market. If a pastoralist tries to grow crops to reduce his dependence on the market, his herding becomes less efficient. The herder tries to pass his farm at least twice a year on his migrations to leave or pick up the farming members of his household. The herder's most effective antidrought strategy is the flexibility of his migration routes; farming clearly interferes or limits this adaptability. But increasing pressure on land has restricted this flexibility anyway, and more and more pastoralists now have farms.

Table 4–A

Adjustment of Food Behavior During Famine

Measures and Specific Actions
Taken by Rural Communities to Cope with Famine

Measures	⬅➡	Specific Action
Adjusting agriculture and animal husbandry		• Planting of famine reserve crops • Resowing (this may be done many times) • Searching for other agricultural lands • Searching for other pastures
Building food stocks		• Hoarding of food • Selling of property for food • Money lending for food
Adjustments of dietary habits		***Reduction of food intakes:*** • Restricting consumption to save food for other people such as children • Reducing number of meals a day • Adding extra water to meals ***Consumption of unconventional foods:*** • Wild plants, fruits, and animals • Cattle fodder • Mixing food with inedible substances • Seed for sowing, slaughter of domestic animals • Anthropophagy (cannibalism) • Eating carrion
Roaming for food		• Begging for food from better-off households • Collecting wild foods • Procuring food from less affected areas • Pillaging for food
Migrating		• Temporary distribution of children to better-off households • Temporary or permanent migration to towns or less affected rural areas
Trying spiritual measures		• Prayer • Magic, rainmaking, witchcraft

Somali pastoralists of the drought-stricken Hararghe province of Ethiopia have developed ways of dealing with famine. Among the methods they use are dividing their herds; redistributing between kinds of animals, cash, or grain; loaning cash or animals; and increasing livestock sales. Under extreme conditions, other measures can include temporary redistribution of children among relatives and, lastly, the use of force against groups competing for the same scarce resources (Seaman, Holt, and Rivers 1974).

Pastoralists tend to build large herds. If the herd is large, they believe, drought or disease may not be able to reduce it below the critical subsistence threshold. Pastoralists are often criticized for having too many animals in normal times. But their behavior reflects their fear of losing animals to drought, particularly when they may need to sell them to buy grain at a time when the price of grain has risen and that of animals has fallen. A household that can sustain itself on five goats in normal times needs more than forty goats to see it through a year when the livestock death rate is 50 percent and the price of grain has increased five times.

Herders also diversify their herds—usually a combination of sheep and goats. This diversification makes it less likely that disease will affect the entire herd. Since different animals require different forage, a mixture is safer in an unpredictable climate. Small stock are also useful, because they are less valuable and can be sold to meet small cash needs. Lending—or even stealing—animals prevents excessive inbreeding and leads to hardier herds (de Waal 1988).

Adjusting Food-consumption Patterns

When faced with a food shortage, most households ration food. Household rationing does not usually lead to increased food prices, but hoarding by traders and shopkeepers hoping for a rise in prices is a widespread phenomenon with dangerous consequences.

Families confronted with famine are forced to restrict the amount of food they consume, in part by cutting back on the number of meals they eat a day. For example, a three-meals-a-day pattern may be reduced to two meals a day or one. In some circumstances, people may eat one meal every other day. These strategies will not relieve the situation much, especially for families that are already malnourished, but they are an indication of food shortage.

People may also dilute meals, such as stew or gruel, with more water. Food may also be mixed with unusual substances such as bark. In some Asian countries, cereal may be mixed with grass seeds.

Use of Famine Foods

Many societies in famine areas have identified alternative foods to eat during times of scarcity. These include wild plants and animals. A study of the plants and animals consumed during food crises in India's Rajasthan Desert identified twenty-five plant species, ranging from trees and shrubs to grasses and annual herbs (Bhandari 1974). In Ethiopia, people eat parts of cactus. In addition, some people grow hardy, less tasteful perennials on lands suitable only for their growth or on sections reserved for hard times.

Many communities may be forced to subsist on nonconventional foods. In India, for example, people in the drier regions of the country may, during scarce times, eat plants that contain woody tissue and substances that are neither digestible nor nutritive. These plants can make people listless or ill, but people eat them, because they temporarily appease hunger.

In the savanna zones of West Africa, a grasslike millet with tiny seeds, called hungry rice (*digitaria exilis*), is often consumed during food shortages. To overcome food-shortage problems, many countries have encouraged the cultivation of famine-reserve crops. Some famine foods, however, present problems. In Mozambique, for example, some strains of cassava proved to have levels of arsenic that were dangerous when only that food was eaten.

When people have to eat the seeds and tubers intended for the next planting season, famine can be prolonged. Famine recurred quickly in Ethiopia after the great famine of 1984–85, in part because many people had to eat their seed reserves. Most food aid imported to Ethiopia in that period was sorghum and wheat from hybrid varieties that cannot regenerate. Since much of the aid arrived after the seed stocks had been eaten, the government had to provide farmers with the seeds for their next crops.

Family Size as a Famine Adjustment

Some populations adjust to famine by having more children, since most famine-vulnerable societies experience high infant-mortality rates. This information is significant: societies that have made major advances in reducing infant mortality are likely to have rapid increases in their populations in a short period. Such increases will strain already overstretched food-production systems.

5 | Early-warning and Monitoring Systems

> The issue is not early warning; it's early response.
>
> Don Krumm, 1983

Introduction

Early warning is the identification and interpretation of events that indicate a famine may be developing. Data can be collected from many sources and used to identify patterns that warn of an impending crisis. Planners can forecast possible scenarios in the affected areas, the access vulnerable groups will have to food supplies, and the extent to which famine conditions may spread.

In reviewing the repetitive crises in Africa in the 1980s, it is clear most relief agencies recognized early signs of developing famine and formal warnings were given through official channels to the international donor community. Yet despite these warnings, reaction was slow. Major news coverage of the disasters—with pictures of mass starvation—were required before international assistance was mobilized. It was not lack of information that caused the international community's slow reaction, but its skepticism of the validity of the information provided, political considerations, and budgetary and administrative constraints. Ethiopia, for example, had a radical socialist government distrusted by the West. At the time that this book was being edited, political considerations were holding up delivery of food to North Korea, although there was clear evidence of an emerging famine.

The biggest limitation on the use of early-warning systems is the fact that most famines occur because of war. During fighting, it is difficult to collect necessary information and to forecast how the conflict will unfold. Most of the theoretical base for the development of warning systems arose out of work being carried out in the famines of the 1970s in areas where there was no fighting. However, it is still possible to apply the early-warning techniques to conflict areas, especially if agencies are working in areas that are effectively controlled by one side or the other. Agencies may also detect what is happening inside an area by gathering data from refugees or displaced people and comparing these facts to information obtained from satellites. Famine-warning systems can also be used to monitor ongoing food emergencies. For this reason, it is important to grasp the fundamentals of the warning systems, how they work, their capabilities, and their limitations.

Purposes

Early warning has two aspects:

- Assessment of vulnerability
- Prediction or early recognition of the triggering events

Identification of Vulnerable Areas

To determine where early-warning systems should be established, areas that have a history of famines need to be identified. If famines have occurred recently, their underlying causes are likely to remain.

The conditions that lead to famines are also easy to identify. These conditions include a high percentage of subsistence farming, extreme ecological changes such as increased desertification or extensive deforestation, economic indicators such as declining household income and increasing household debt, and high incidence of infant mortality and morbidity. While one of these conditions alone is not serious enough to make an area vulnerable to famine, the presence of several is.

Famine-monitoring systems should be established in all areas where the most common famine triggers—drought and widespread civil conflict—are occurring.

Regions where other famine triggers exist should also be automatically monitored. These include areas of widespread insect infestation, especially locusts; regions where agriculture is dependent on rain-fed irrigation and seasonal rainfall is subject to extreme variations; and territories bordering on economic collapse such as Haiti.

In rare cases, changes in political policy trigger famines, as in China during the Great Leap Forward, or they are caused by other forces that quickly reduce the number of farmers in an area.

Areas where vulnerable conditions are prevalent should be delineated and mapped, a process called *vulnerability mapping*. Were a famine to occur, these maps would be used to plan programs and plot the geographic extent and shift of the famine. The maps can be important in planning logistical support. They can also be used to help determine the measures to be taken to contain the spread of the famine in adjoining areas. (See Figure 5–1, Figure 5–2, and Table 5–A.)

Figure 5-1

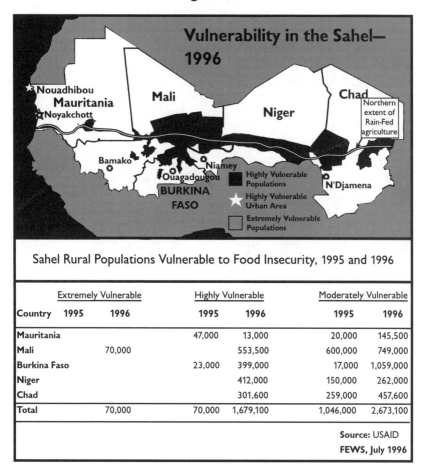

Sahel Rural Populations Vulnerable to Food Insecurity, 1995 and 1996					
	Extremely Vulnerable		Highly Vulnerable		Moderately Vulnerable	
Country	1995	1996	1995	1996	1995	1996
Mauritania			47,000	13,000	20,000	145,500
Mali		70,000		553,500	600,000	749,000
Burkina Faso			23,000	399,000	17,000	1,059,000
Niger				412,000	150,000	262,000
Chad				301,600	259,000	457,600
Total		70,000	70,000	1,679,100	1,046,000	2,673,100

Source: USAID
FEWS, July 1996

Famine Indicators

Until recently, famines were assessed in terms of medical cases, rates or degrees of malnutrition, and/or numbers of deaths from malnutrition and disease. Such indicators quantify the suffering that has already taken place and thus are called *trailing indicators*. They are of limited use in predicting and preventing famine.

Famine warning systems sometimes rely more heavily on trailing indicators than data or indicators that precede, or lead, a famine. This happens, in part, because trailing indicators are easier to detect and monitor than leading ones. In addition, monitoring *leading indicators* requires a sophisticated system of data collection and analysis. Factors such as political instability, economic crisis, and income decline require advanced analytical tools.

Figure 5-2

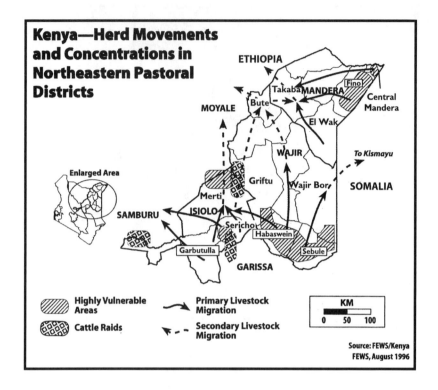

Kenya—Herd Movements and Concentrations in Northeastern Pastoral Districts

Source: FEWS/Kenya
FEWS, August 1996

Famine Early-warning Systems

In recent years, there has been a proliferation of famine early-warning systems (FEWSs). On an international level, the two most important are the Famine Early Warning System (also FEWS), sponsored by the U.S. Agency for International Development (USAID), and the Global Information and Early Warning System of the Food and Agricultural Organisation (FAO), a UN agency. Two programs give region-wide assistance in the Sahel. The Agricultural/Hydrological/Meteorological Program provides data collection and analysis, and a European Union project furnishes FEWS statistical assistance in the countries organized under the Comite Inter-Etat Pour la Lutte Contre la Secheresse au Sahel. Several countries have established their own famine early-warning systems, and a number of nongovernmental organizations (NGOs) have also set up systems. Each varies according to the factors monitored and the responses they trigger.

Each system is unique; the differences reflect the requirements of the country that is being monitored. In some cases, they differ in the approaches used to link the warning indicators with specific responses.

Table 5-A
Indicators for Action

INDICATORS OF VULNERABILITY

- Subsistence cultivation
- Recurring rainfall shortages
- Heavy debt burden among farmers
- Low food reserves
- Political instability
- Farmers required to work part time off their lands
- Increasing desertification, soil erosion, or deforestation
- Increasing salinity of soils

INDICATORS OF IMMINENT CRISIS

- Prolonged drought
- Onset of a natural disaster (floods, insect infestation, et cetera)
- Crop failure
- Increased price of staples
- Rise in price ratio of staple grain to prevailing wages
- Increase in lending rates in the informal lending sector
- Increase in sales of livestock and decrease in average sale price
- Increased distress sales
- Increase in deaths among livestock
- Unusual sales of possessions such as jewelry, ornaments, et cetera
- Seed shortage or increased cost of seeds
- Widespread sales of land at abnormally low prices
- Increased hoarding of grains by dealers
- Consumption of animals by pastoralists
- Consumption of famine foods

INDICATORS OF FAMINE (TRAILING INDICATORS)

- Increased rates of death
- Migration
- Some family members going to urban areas to work
- Increased rates of low or abnormal growth in children
- Increased rates of famine-related disease such as measles
- Edema in young children
- Increased rates of vitamin deficiencies
- Increased rates of nutritional disorders
- Sale of traction animals such as oxen
- Consumption of seeds

Types of Warning Systems

Most famine early-warning systems focus on trigger mechanisms, using food-supply and food-demand models as predictors. This is logical: accurate predictions of the timing of a famine cannot be made until the trigger event occurs. Only the increasing possibility of famine is evident.

Food-supply models use national harvest predictions and measurements of stored food and food imports, balanced against expected national food consumption, to assess whether sufficient food will be available in a country. This approach, known as the food balance sheet, is often too simplistic to be applied universally. Too many factors intervene between the existence of food in a country and its consumption by those who need it. Such models cannot, for example, take into account food stored in private rather than public hands or the role played by food merchants.

Food-demand models recognize these intervening factors. They do not try to measure how much food is available. Instead, they attempt to find out whether people have reasonable access to that food. Access is measured by the market price and whether people have the money to buy an item or something to barter for it. A rapid increase in food prices and/or a drop in family income may indicate the onset of famine. This approach does not necessarily contradict the availability approach but provides a framework for understanding famines caused by food-production failure and other economic or political factors. This model can be applied to more areas, since it is not tied to one trigger mechanism. Furthermore, it has the potential to locate both the geographical area of famine and those social groups that will suffer most.

Food-demand systems have limitations. Often, market data are not subjective. For example, livestock can be sold and resold in a village market a number of times in one day. Therefore, figures for livestock sales and prices may not reflect the income the original seller got for his animals. Equally, grain prices are usually recorded by the sack, but the famine victim buys food by the cupful at a unit price that may be many times higher than the quoted market price (Walker 1987).

A number of observers argue that most famine-warning systems are mechanisms that allow people outside a society to look inside. The systems, they point out, are structured to gather information that will improve the efficiency of externally derived and controlled relief measures. These critics contend that neither approach helps prevent the famine or suggests effective forms of relief that will decrease the vulnerability of the society to famine in the future (Devereux and Hay 1986).

To achieve these broader aims, a FEWS must look at what causes a community and its members to be vulnerable to famine; how the coping mechanisms that have evolved can be strengthened; and what alternative strategies, based on that community's viewpoint, can be adopted (Walker 1987).

FEWS should aim to do three things:

- Define the most effective counterfamine interventions and identify the locations where they should be applied

- Put the relief structures in a country on alert, so they are able to cope with the relief needs if they are necessary

- Provide the information needed to effectively lobby donors so that the required assistance arrives in time (Walker 1987)

Sudan Early Warning System (EWS)

The Sudan EWS is a national system using secondary data. It does not collect its own information. To identify areas facing food crises, EWS collects data that affect food and markets: meteorological, nutritional, and agricultural-progress facts. First, historical and current information is examined to establish the context within which change is occurring. When areas of stress are detected, the staff conducts surveys in those areas to verify a problem exists. If the surveys indicate a food or market problem, further studies are taken to quantify assistance requirements. Governmental and nongovernmental groups within Sudan provide the initial data. The main problem with this system is its lack of effectiveness in identifying pockets of need.

Botswana Early Warning and Response System

The Botswana Early Warning and Response System is designed to initiate relief programs as soon as stress is detected in preidentified vulnerable areas. Rainfall/agro-meteorological data and crop forecasts/grazing conditions trigger operations. The program is designed to begin promptly at the time a failed harvest would be gathered. Nutritional surveillance is used as a monitoring and targeting tool, not an early-warning indicator. NGOs provide little, if any, data to the EWS, since their presence in Botswana is limited.

Kenyan Plan Against Drought and Famine in Turkana

As a result of a severe drought and food shortages in Kenya's Turkana district, the government and OXFAM developed a drought-contingency plan modeled on the Indian famine codes of the 1900s. It consists of a district drought policy and a group of advanced preparations and sets up a rudimentary FEWS. The plan lays out actions to be taken by government authorities during a drought to ensure food availability, to guarantee employment for destitute people via public works, and to buy animals from herders at reasonable prices (to help maintain their purchasing power). It also specifies rural reconstruction measures for use after the drought. A district drought-contingency officer coordinates the measures. Other strategies are suggested to reinforce the regional plan, including: advanced negotiation of commitments from donors; construction of infrastructure such as stores, roads, et cetera; technical training seminars for district and governmental staff; and standardization of nutritional-surveillance techniques.

The systems in Botswana and northern Kenya are geared to activate counterfamine programs and create barriers against famine with employment-guarantee schemes and other food-aid programs. Systems that focus on social security rather than solely on food relief require different organization and information from those systems designed to guide traditional relief efforts.

Systeme d'Alerte Precoce (SAP)

Since 1984, Médecins sans Frontières/Belgium (MSF) has worked on information systems based on its rapid nutritional assessment system (the score system, as it is called). This FEWS effort is designed to develop data that can help governments prevent food crises, and MSF and the Association pour le Developement Economique et Santa have provided technical assistance to the national authorities in Mali and Chad to establish a national FEWS.

The FEWS has organized within national governments and their regional offices. It is complementary to existing systems used to develop national food-balance estimates by comparing the total food available with the food needs of the population.

The project focuses on the traditional at-risk zones in the two countries. In Mali, it covers the northern and the northwestern parts of the country, or approximately four million people.

The main objectives of the FEWS are:

- To detect and predict food shortages and affected populations, i.e., to figure out the number at risk

- To inform national authorities and international organizations of a developing crisis, when a response should be made, and what actions are necessary and possible to prevent or solve the problem

SAP—Niger

The response to droughts and famine in 1968–69 and 1972–73 led the Niger government to improve infrastructure for response to famine and organize committees to set up monitoring. The famine of 1984–85 stimulated further committees to provide early warning and a response capacity. The current system involves institutions created by the Niger government through various decrees since 1989. The Niger government administers the system, but it is primarily dependent on donor funds for operation. SAP has created a number of government offices to study and compile data across sectors (nutrition, crop production, rainfall, pest infestation, and so on). Most government projections of need are based on national cereal balances. Technical analysis of needs has been generally ineffective as local SAP staff members are often insecure about data sources and analysis, as are donors. SAP structure typically lacks resources and motivation, but SAP has been able to respond during food crises.

SAP—Chad

The Chad SAP is also an institutional one administered by the government, and like the program in Niger, it suffers from resource poverty. However, the government and donors have developed a system to jointly collect, analyze, and agree on data and their use, giving both institutional strength to SAP and confidence in analysis and action. A committee on which donors and a representative of the USAID FEWS project sit oversees the SAP program.

Save the Children Fund (United Kingdom)

In 1986, Save the Children, in conjunction with the London School of Hygiene and Tropical Medicine, set up a network that would gather information that could be used to predict future drought and famine. The system is based in the four districts of the Mopti region in central Mali and seeks to make famine mitigation a partnership between village-level leadership and national and international partners.

Village field workers collect data on such indicators as rainfall, crop and livestock production, food prices, and malnutrition levels. The project publishes a local journal that shares findings and successes. A quarterly journal also gives information to government and international partners. Local coping mechanisms such as cultivation of wild famine foods and traditional water conservation are also encouraged through local credit programs and support for local women's projects.

Many aspects of the project were discontinued in 1995, but at the time this book was being edited, Save the Children was in the process of restarting the program.

OXFAM Early Warning System

The goal of the OXFAM EWS in Mali is to "try to develop a famine monitoring response strategy for a *cercle* (subdistrict administrative unit)." An emphasis is put on the development of the capacity of the local community to respond to and control what happens in its locality. This approach is looking for an alternative way of responding to a crisis rather than following the usual process of providing emergency aid at a late stage. It is an example of a local participation-focused program that takes into account the indigenous view of the situation and what was needed in response to a local crisis.

The OXFAM EWS is based on four premises:

- Famine develops over several years. Therefore, it should be possible to identify early signs of food crisis at a local level well before emergency aid is needed.

- Early-warning information and response should be integrated, so the agency collecting data should be able to act on it

- The response should reinforce the population's ability to face a crisis rather than providing only emergency aid

- Local populations should play a role in collecting data

The OXFAM EWS is based on its project partners—cereal banks, cooperatives, and associations. Groups are asked to collect rainfall and market data four times a year. OXFAM personnel then collect this information in the region and discuss the current situation, proposing interventions, if necessary.

Another aspect of this project is to further research the local-level dynamics of early-warning indicators. Currently work is being carried out in livestock prices.

The project staff identified several limitations to this approach. A project covers a small geographical area and thus a limited number of people. There is the risk of local populations distorting data to gain assistance. A continuation of data collection can be ensured after the project ends or when there is a series of good years.

6 | *Approaches to Famine Relief*

Introduction

Famine interventions fall into two categories:

- Conventional relief, which provides food and a few other items directly to famine victims
- Counterfamine efforts, a variety of economic actions or agricultural-support activities taken to stabilize local markets and to increase poor people's ability to buy or grow the food they need or to obtain it through alternative methods. Counterfamine efforts usually rely on existing market systems.

Conventional Relief

Conventional famine relief usually consists of three elements:

- Food and/or vitamins
- A variety of health-care and public-health-assistance programs
- Such support as temporary shelter, water, and sanitation facilities to settlements and camps where migration has occurred

Food-aid programs usually provide rations to families. When conditions are severe, supplementary foods are also distributed to vulnerable groups. Relief agencies often use special foods such as blended grains, vitamin-reinforced flours, and high-protein products.

Famines caused by war or civil conflict almost always require conventional-relief strategies in their early stages, especially for refugees and displaced people who have fled to relief camps or temporary settlements and are unable or not permitted to find jobs. Conventional strategies are also frequently used in the advanced stages of famine.

Overall, conventional relief is *not* successful in controlling early high mortality unless there is ample food in the country at the start of the operation that can be bought or used. Most food aid is imported from the major grain-producing countries, and it can take up to six months to purchase and ship that food and set up a distribution system.

Early studies indicate that the chances of saving lives at the outset of an operation are greatly reduced when food is imported. By the time it arrives in the country and gets to people, many will have died. Evidence suggests the massive food shipments sent to Ethiopia in 1985 had little impact on the outcome of the famine. It took four to six months for the food to arrive in the country, and by the time it arrived in sufficient, steady quantities in the rural areas, the death rate had peaked and was already declining—evidence that those who were most at risk of dying had already perished. For this reason, as well as others discussed below, some relief specialists believe continued emphasis on procuring, shipping, and distributing food from surplus-producing nations is not only unwarranted as the primary famine intervention but possibly risky.

In recent years, relief agencies have streamlined their systems, so conventional food-aid responses have been more effective. USAID now requires a response in no less than three months. In some instances, WFP has responded in less time.

If a conventional-relief program is to be successful, it requires:

- A nearby and available source of food
- The capacity to transport and distribute food
- Most important, an early decision to use this strategy instead of others

Counterfamine Interventions

Counterfamine actions are designed to prevent the famine from developing into an extended emergency and to limit its geographical spread. Such measures attempt to do this by increasing income and food for the poorest people and by attacking the underlying causes of people's poverty. These interventions are aimed at keeping the local market system from collapsing, preventing people from having to sell their assets, stopping migration, and maintaining the family.

The actions, which should start in the early stages of famine, include:

- Income-transfer programs
- Support for existing market systems
- Interventions to maintain transportation systems

- Interventions to maintain rural-trade patterns
- Investments in increasing household economic assets
- Investments in community infrastructure that will support agricultural production

Until recently, famine-relief workers believed counterfamine interventions like these would work only in famines outside conflict zones, especially those that take a long time to develop, such as drought-triggered famines. However, a number of measures associated with this approach were used successfully in northwestern Somalia in 1989 and the liberated areas of the northern Ethiopian war zones in 1990. In 1992, the U.S. government made market interventions its primary relief strategy for the famine sparked by the Somali civil war.

The sole prerequisite for counterfamine interventions is a ready supply of cash and food aid that can be used in unconventional ways, such as direct sales to the victims or to food traders and merchants. A well-organized information-collection system with the capabilities of a famine early-warning system also helps in targeting the specific interventions. (See Chapter 5.)

Conventional Relief Versus Counterfamine Interventions

Which strategy is more effective? Conventional famine relief will always be required, but there is growing confidence that the counterfamine approach is more effective than conventional relief in containing famine and combating malnutrition in the long term. But full-scale counterfamine operations have not been widely used, because most relief agencies and the public have not understood the underlying causes of famine, the reasons people are vulnerable, and the alternate opportunities available.

There is another reason counterfamine efforts are not widespread. Major donor countries have an excess of food, not cash, and their food-aid policies are designed, in part, to support their own agricultural production. The electorate of a donor country is usually inclined to believe that food is less subject to diversion and corruption than programs supported with cash—an assumption that has proven untrue in many instances. Consider the position of a typical relief-agency official in a country where famine conditions have developed. If he/she chooses to use counterfamine measures, he/she probably will have to raise the money through his/her agency. This usually means soliciting donations from the public and requesting grants from major donor governments. Public appeals can take months, and they often do not work until the agency can show photographs of severely malnourished persons—people near death. If the relief official requests money from donor governments, the amount of cash available may be small, rarely more than a million dollars.

However, if the relief official approaches a major grain-exporting country, he/she might get millions of dollars worth of food, as well as the money to administer and monitor its distribution and to buy trucks and fuel for distributing it.

The choice is usually an easy one. The average relief official will choose the latter course. For this reason, today's famine-relief strategies are said to be *food driven* as opposed to *need driven*.

However, counterfamine strategies are becoming more acceptable because of the large number of local-currency reserves now held jointly by the donor country and the host country. These reserves have accumulated from the sale of food and other commodities under aid agreements. These monies, known as counterpart funds, can often be used in emergencies. Furthermore, it is increasingly possible to obtain permission to sell donated foods that are inappropriate for use in the famine to raise cash to buy foods that can be *monetized*, that is, sold to local merchants. These funds can then support income generation in famine areas through work programs, buy and move food available locally, or finance any combination of other appropriate cash-based counterfamine measures.

Counterfamine Operations

7 | Preemptive and Containment Strategies

Introduction

Counterfamine measures are used to prevent famines or stop them from spreading. They can be applied as soon as a situation begins to deteriorate. If actions can be initiated before events get out of hand, a range of strategies is available that can not only preempt the famine but assist the affected communities and families with development rather than relief aid. These measures will have more impact than crisis interventions that may be required once a famine becomes pronounced.

Counterfamine strategies work best in the early stages. Once events excelerate, interventions that rely heavily on food relief will predominate. In the normal realm of famine-relief operations, development assistance is usually given lower priority than food relief, especially during conflicts. Therefore, it is important that counterfamine operations begin as soon as a problem is detected.

Counterfamine interventions are based on the premise that employment and income are the central issues that must be addressed in a famine. If sufficient income can be provided to families, they will not need to liquidate family assets and their ability to purchase food can be restored. If sufficient cash is provided—for example, through cash-for-work projects—and people's purchasing power is maintained, the market will respond and food will be brought into the area. Assistance should be directed toward those activities that will lead to a sustained rise in rural income as well as encourage people to use their earnings to continue their farming or other productive enterprises. If the famine largely stems from a reduction in agricultural production—and if this can be corrected by subsidizing agricultural inputs such as seed and harvest assistance—programs that address these needs are effective preemptive interventions.

A multitude of diverse, small-scale activities should be spread throughout the vulnerable areas. Usually, the number of projects and the rapidity with which they must be implemented is beyond the capacity of any government or relief agency to execute through the normal project-planning and implementation process. The best alternative is to place as much of the responsibility for planning and the resources for carrying out the projects in the hands of the communities and affected families.

The Elements of a Counterfamine Strategy

A counterfamine strategy should address the causes as well as the effects of famine. Families that have lost their incomes require alternative earnings. Thus, agencies should undertake projects designed to:

- Create alternative sources of income and promote a sustained increase in average family earnings
- Prevent a decrease in the value of family assets, especially livestock
- Rehabilitate local markets and fill them with food that is affordable to most of the poor

Agencies can also promote people's investment in activities such as gardening or milk production that make it possible for the most vulnerable families to expand the range of foods they consume, develop skills that will enable them to diversify their sources of income, and, where possible, reduce the vulnerability of their cultivation and livestock practices.

Counterfamine activities can be designed to achieve multiple objectives. They can use the principal resource—labor—most abundant during a famine. They can address the most immediate effect of famine, an overwhelming increase in the number of unemployed people. They can provide income by paying, preferably in cash, for work. And they can prevent the development of a full-blown famine if put in place in time and in the areas where people live.

When properly planned, counterfamine measures can prevent the social and economic disintegration that accompanies mass migrations of people searching for food and the pattern of dependency that often develops when food aid is handed out free.

Counterfamine actions are divided into two sets of economic interventions: income-support projects and market interventions.

Income-support Projects

A number of programs, called *income-support projects*, can be set up in the famine zone to provide the poor with cash to help restore their purchasing power. Wages are paid principally in cash. Cash, in-kind grants, and, where possible, loans may also be used to inject resources into the community.

Although counterfamine strategy depends on employment generation and cash-for-work projects, it differs in a number of significant respects from conventional public-works schemes. The majority of the projects should focus on improving the productivity of the lands, crops, or livestock herds and rehabilitating the market and food-distribution system. Priority should be given to paying people to improve their own assets, particularly land. While a road-building project may help the community and can certainly create income for workers, it will not do much toward reducing the vulnerability of area farms to drought and crop failures. The projects should also develop ways for communities to decrease their collective vulnerability to famines by establishing such things as community-based food banks. The projects must be designed to yield rapid returns. This is essential if the projects are to result in immediate protection for the poor and reduce their vulnerability to famine. An important aspect of the projects is the mobilization of community labor. These projects should use traditional labor-organization techniques or institute cooperative-labor schemes that villagers can continue after the crisis. People should be involved in organizing and structuring the labor force, and the normal lines of authority should be respected.

It is critical that the projects not divert labor from essential agricultural activities. If projects must be carried out during times when people are fully occupied with their usual work, the activities can be organized so they can be interrupted to allow people to work their land or to work on a part-time basis.

The Role of Food Aid

The counterfamine approach does not exclude the need for food aid. Some households will probably require supplementary food, especially families living at the margins of the famine zones. Strategies that employ alternative food-for-work schemes may be required to increase food supplies in some areas. (See Chapter 10.)

Some families may need to receive free food supplements, but these should be limited to people who are most in need. The mere perception that free food is available can create expectations that can undermine other intervention strategies. Furthermore, if food aid is not targeted properly, large portions may end up being sold on the market and could contribute to food-price fluctuations that could have a negative impact in the community.

Generally, food aid serves two purposes. First, it can be used as the equivalent of income for families who have lost their normal source of funds. Second, it can be used to finance, or partly finance, relief or rehabilitation activities. Food aid should be limited, so that supply does not exceed demand—otherwise it will push prices too low for food producers to make a profit and thereby retard agricultural recovery. In general, this means that food aid should only be used if it is clear the local market cannot meet the demand for food—in other words, that famine is developing as a result of food, not income, deficiencies.

When food is being supplied from abroad, it is usually preferable to exchange the imported food for locally purchased food, if it is available. This helps maintain a demand for locally produced food and can result in major savings in transport costs.

It is important to understand food aid from the beneficiary's viewpoint. Most relief personnel see food aid as an alternate source of food for starving families. The recipients, however, view it in a broader context. They see it as income and a transfer of assets. Since the majority of people are farmers who normally sell food for income, receiving food from a relief agency is like receiving cash. Even in the most extreme circumstances, people will barter relief food for other commodities or needed services. It is not unusual to find people selling food for water, household items such as soap, other foods such as spices or salt, and for essential services such as grain milling.

For these reasons, food aid distributed to meet a nutritional target rather than income security is likely to reduce the family's overall ability to recover both its income and food security.

Market Interventions

Many agencies view the selling of emergency food aid with alarm. This attitude, however, tends to restrict the use of food as a general resource with broad applications, and it limits support for the kinds of activities central to a counterfamine and containment strategy.

There are many situations where the sale of food is desirable, even when the food supply is inadequate to meet demands. When supplies are scarce, there is a corresponding increase in food prices that erodes the purchasing power of the poorest families. Giving food away will not reduce the food crisis. People need to sell food, creating a surplus that will bring market prices down.

The distribution of free food rations requires that a major logistical supply system be developed at great cost. Such systems can rarely be put in place rapidly, and lives are endangered while they are being set up. In such cases, it would be simpler to sell food aid, using the normal markets as the distribution system. There is no reason food aid cannot be sold to local traders, especially the microentrepreneurs such as women vendors, who usually sell their own produce in the markets. If enough food is sold to a large number of small vendors, it is unlikely that any one vendor will hoard sufficient food to drive up the price. These local traders will usually resell food aid at prices affordable to the poor. Furthermore, these sales generate funds that can be used to help finance cash-for-work projects. Thus, sales achieve multiple objectives—cash for the counterfamine projects and support for the small traders.

An example of how this can work is the program initiated by CARE in western Sudan in 1990. It consisted of the following activities:

- *Market Interventions.* CARE wanted to revitalize village markets, its primary action. Supplies of grain were procured and delivered to village councils, where they were sold at subsidized prices to the small retail vendors in the market. The selling price was initially equivalent to the previous year's highest wholesale figure. Sales were limited, and purchasers had to agree to sell their grains within a certain range, roughly equivalent to the previous year's retail-sales price, adjusted for inflation (approximately 200 to 250 Sudanese pounds, or $5 per sack). The amount sold to each vendor was limited, and the retail market was monitored to ensure vendors sold the grain within the agreed limits. Any vendor found selling above that level or to wholesale merchants was disqualified from subsequent sales.

  Proceeds from the sales were assigned to village councils to organize cash-for-work projects. Families that could not afford to buy grain even at the depressed price were given priority for employment in the cash-for-work projects. Projects were selected by the village council and monitored by NGOs assigned to the area.

- *Food Loans.* In the initial stages, sufficient cash-for-work projects were difficult to organize to meet the needs of all families whose convertible assets had been sold. Rather than giving food away, families were loaned food and had an obligation to repay it into a village food bank in increments during the next good harvest.

- *Food for Work.* Food-for-work programs were initiated in towns and other areas where large numbers of migrants accumulated. The programs were also carried out in the peripheral areas of the food-deficit zone, those communities where harvests were reduced no more than 50 percent of normal. If losses were more than 50 percent, direct-aid programs were used.

- *Price Supports for Livestock.* A program of interventions designed to increase prices of livestock was carried out in Sudan, using local-currency accounts from major donor nations. Interventions included buying livestock at fair prices, redirecting livestock away from towns and urban centers (the long-haul lorries that brought food to the area were used to take sheep and goats back to Port Sudan for export, bypassing the Khartoum market), and in certain cases, purchasing goats and redistributing them among the rural poor whose herds had been depleted.

- *Food Supplements.* NGOs instituted a program for identifying people or groups that required emergency nutritional support such as the elderly, lactating women, and children under five years of age who were immediately threatened.

As a result of these interventions, famine conditions were contained and the markets functioned normally until the end of the drought.

Market interventions can also work in conflict zones. An example is the program launched by USAID during the drought/civil war in Somalia in 1992. Donors gave food to the WFP, which transferred it to CARE. CARE representatives in Kenya sold and delivered food to Somali traders, who then took it to the famine zone and resold it to small retail vendors. By traveling at night and by using pack animals, armed convoys, friendships, clan affiliations, or business relationships, the traders were able to travel safely through contested areas to reach villages that were largely inaccessible to relief agencies. The proceeds of the sales were transferred to NGOs working in the area to use in a variety of income-generating projects as well as agricultural rehabilitation. The increased sources of income had two important effects:

- They increased the purchasing power of those in danger of having severe nutritional problems
- They created a more attractive market for merchants who sold WFP/CARE food as well as other previously reserved stocks

Uses of Food Aid to Support Market Interventions

Food aid can be used in other ways to support local-trade patterns. Three innovative methods are payment-in-kind (PiK) programs, animal-grain exchanges for pastoralists, and barter schemes.

- *The PiK Program.* PiK programs are designed to help support local farmers and to maintain the normal market system. Farmers are paid in grains to improve their land with counterdrought or counterdesertification methods such as contouring, terracing, or planting wind breaks and for participating in community-development projects such as developing water-harvesting measures. Instead of receiving wages, farmers obtain payment in grain equivalent to the amount they would have produced under normal conditions. If their harvest has totally failed, they collect the full amount. If they harvest a percentage of their normal yield, they are paid the balance.

Supporters of PiK programs cite a number of advantages. These programs allow farmers to manage their crops as they see fit, without having to sell everything, including the next year's seed reserve. The recipient can use grain received in the PiK program to barter for other goods, returning near-normal conditions to the market. Since PiK programs work substantially through market mechanisms, requirements for relief-agency management are considerably less.

While PiK programs can be used throughout a famine zone, they are most effective in stabilizing grain markets on the periphery of drought-affected areas and for countering the development of famine conditions in isolated food-deficit areas. They are especially useful in places where only small farmers are experiencing shortages.

As a famine-control measure, PiK programs are effective in countering famine shifts. Like all counterfamine measures, however, the programs should not develop a life of their own. PiK programs also have the potential to deflate grain prices at the time of harvest or discourage production in other ways. (See Chapter 10 for a more detailed discussion of the PiK program.)

- *Grain for Animal Exchanges.* Providing relief grain in exchange for animals at fair prices achieves two objectives:

  - It preserves the value of animals and the pastoralist's income

  - If the animals can be slaughtered and the meat preserved, the project transforms deteriorating food stocks into food reserves

- *Barter.* Grain can often be used as barter for more appropriate foods or seeds and agricultural inputs. For example, wheat, which has a relatively high value in many countries, may be bartered for sorghum or other lower-value grains at exchange ratios that increase the amount of food available for use in the relief program. When wheat is available, wealthier consumers purchase it, reducing demand on less prestigious grains and effectively reducing prices for poorer consumers.

Other Strategies for Increasing Access to Food

Releasing Government-held Food Stocks

One strategy that governments use to increase food supplies and to decrease prices is the release of government-held food into the private market.

Sales at Controlled Prices

Governments often establish outlets for selling food at regulated prices to the poor. An example is the fair-price shops in India during the Bihar drought of 1966–67, when the government set up over 20,000 stores (Berg 1971). Such approaches guarantee supplies to those with limited incomes.

Related to this option is the free or subsidized distribution of special rations to specific classes of people—women with dependent children, the sick, and the elderly—who cannot otherwise obtain food.

Food Subsidies

In the 1960s, Sri Lanka implemented a guaranteed food-subsidy program. Under this scheme, each low-income family received food stamps that could be redeemed for free rice rations weekly. The rations provided slightly less than the minimum requirements for a balanced diet, so the program was considered a supplement to what a family could buy. Such a program had its costs—both fiscally and socially. But the subsidy program improved food security for the poor. Food stamps were credited with substantially reducing the risk of famine among displaced populations during the country's long civil war.

Countries with long-term food-subsidy and distribution schemes are better prepared to face major food shortages. Clearly, design of a subsidy program is a complex task, but overall, it is a good strategy to consider.

Price Controls

Price controls are often proposed to ensure the poor's access to food. In most cases, however, controls have been a failure, and in many cases, they create a black market or, worse, result in food being hoarded or smuggled to other areas.

Most of these mechanisms are applicable once a famine has entered late second and third stages (Cutler's model, Figure 1–3 in Chapter 1) and are discussed in more detail in Chapter 10.

Targeting Counterfamine Measures

Commonly, three situations are encountered in the early stages of famine:

- *The loss of agricultural incomes in areas where it is possible to increase or at least resume normal production by making land improvements and introducing improved farming or animal husbandry techniques.* In these cases, the priorities are mobilizing labor for land improvements, constructing or rehabilitating irrigation systems, improving drainage, reducing erosion, et cetera.

- *The loss of agricultural incomes in areas where land is scarce and not everyone will be able to resume production at the previous level.* This situation may have developed as the result of poor land management, expanded population pressure, desertification, or increased soil salinity. The priority is to identify families that require alternative sources of income. Work can be developed by providing start-up capital for new enterprises and extensive training in new skills.

- *A situation where large population migrations have occurred and agriculture cannot provide a stable source of income for the majority of people.* Emphasis can be placed on providing long-term alternative sources of income. In some cases, the government may propose resettling people to more productive areas. The measure is often socially disruptive, leading to tension and conflict that ultimately will increase income insecurity.

Tables 7–A and 7–B summarize some of the types of projects that can be used to counter the development and spread of famine conditions.

Proper targeting of counterfamine aid is critical to a successful program. Often relief agencies fail to select the correct beneficiaries for projects or overlook key aspects of a society that play a factor in the outcome of the project. A common example of poor targeting occurs in the projects that use food- or cash-for-work programs. The projects often simply build public infrastructures rather than focus on improving the farmers' lands or increasing output on subsistence plots. As a result, the impact is limited to the provision of income or food support.

Food-for-work programs have a checkered history in targeting beneficiaries. Care must be exercised to ensure that people working are from the families most in need and that food reaches family members with the greatest necessities.

Some counterfamine technical-assistance programs have failed, because the intended recipients of assistance were incorrectly identified. This often occurs when relief agencies focus their attention exclusively on men. They assume that men, as the heads of households, usually make critical decisions about food production. In many societies, however, women decide questions concerning the growing of subsistence foods. This is especially true where food and cash crops are grown simultaneously. Women tend to look after the fields where they grow subsistence foods, while men manage cash crops. Alex de Waal reported that in western Sudan, "even on farms which are jointly managed by husband and wife, the man is usually solely responsible for major cash crops such as ground nuts and sesame, while the woman spends most of her time in the fields working on the grain crop" (Hay 1986).

Issues in Counterfamine Operations

Political Obstacles to Counterfamine Approaches

Perhaps the most difficult obstacles to overcome when planning a counterfamine program are political ones. Political constraints are usually obvious: they come in the form of government policies, inflexible program guidelines that seem etched in stone, and bureaucratic procedures that make innovation all but impossible. If the famine is in a

Table 7-A

Intervention to Counter the Development and Spread of Famine

Type of Intervention ◄►	Methods (In Order of Priority)
• Income Support	• Cash for Work 　Temporary Jobs 　PiK 　Coupon-store Approach 　Food for Work 　Cash Grants 　Direct Food Aid
• Price Supports for 　Cultivators and Pastoralists	• Animal-grain Exchanges • Subsidized Purchases
• Consumer/Market Support	• Subsidized Sales of Food Through 　Microvendors in Local Markets • Subsidized Sales of Food in National Markets

---

Table 7-B
Income-support Projects

DIRECT INVESTMENTS
- Land improvements (contouring, terracing, soil improvements)
- Erosion control (planting trees for windbreaks, erecting sand fences, et cetera)
- Irrigation improvements
- Alternative crops (distribution of seeds)
- Crop salvaging (alternative uses of stunted crops, that is, fodder)
- Construction of on-farm grain-storage facilities
- Distribution of replacement seeds, fertilizers, pesticides

INDIRECT INVESTMENTS
- Town-market improvements
- Farm-to-market road construction
- Construction of cooperative grain-storage facilities
- Construction or improvement of public water systems
- Subsidized local farm-implement manufacturing

LOWER-PRIORITY PROJECTS
- Construction of schools, market structures, health facilities

---

conflict zone, political obstacles may prove formidable.

There are many hidden political agendas that make a counterfamine program difficult to accomplish. These usually occur at the international level and involve relations between donors and the affected country. A good example occurred during the Ethiopian famine in 1986. The primary food aid donor was the U.S. government. Due to political hostilities between Ethiopia and the United States, American assistance was limited to humanitarian aid. A Congressional ban prohibited development assistance. The U.S. mission in Addis Ababa interpreted this ban to mean that assistance was limited to providing food directly to the famine victims—approaches such as cash for work were strictly prohibited. Such political obstacles only penalize the poor and are shortsighted.

Doctrinal Obstacles to Counterfamine Approaches

Some formidable obstacles are doctrinal: policies set up with good intentions that are, in practice, counterproductive. Relief agencies abound in them. For example, food given by donors is usually restricted to free distribution.

Other donors have established artificial classifications for their assistance, dividing aid into *relief* and *development*. Unfortunately, many of the more important counterfamine approaches have been classified as development aid, making them unavailable or bureaucratically difficult to use in emergencies.

The biggest doctrinal obstacles, however, stem from the limited understanding people have about the processes at play in famines. For example, a common attitude holds that people who are in distress should not have to pay for food. Thus, many agencies are unwilling to use cash-for-work approaches.

Doctrines spring out of "conventional wisdom" or long-held beliefs about famines. If people are starving, it is assumed there is a food shortage, so food is imported. Few look for food in the famine zone and thus miss the opportunity to buy food locally or support local agricultural prices and speed the famine-relief process.

Until the origins of famine are faced for what they are and the cause-and-effect relations are more clearly understood, relief agencies will continue to bind themselves to inappropriate, expensive, and largely ineffective responses.

8 | *Income-generating Projects*

During counterfamine operations, relief workers must initiate projects designed to provide alternative sources of income to the most affected families. To have a long-term, developmental impact, projects can be designed to help the most vulnerable farmers. When planning projects, several principles should be followed:

- Priority should be given to projects that have a direct, immediate impact on improving agricultural production or reducing farmers' losses

- Projects should be organized on a communal and cooperative basis and should be labor intensive, creating as much income as possible. Projects that need a large percentage of the cost of the project for equipment or capital outlay should be avoided.

- Projects should provide a sustained and fair, but not high, wage

- Projects should be carried out in a way that will help preserve peoples' dignity, confidence, and self-esteem

- Projects should not compete with or draw resources away from normal agricultural production activities

Project Categories

Projects can be divided into three categories: individual projects on farms, mutual-help projects for small groups of farmers, and projects that benefit the community.

On-farm Projects

Many projects can be designed as self-help activities, and relief agencies can encourage farmers to make improvements to their land. To pay people to carry out these activities may seem counterproductive and may lead to concerns they will create dependencies. However, the practice is common in developed countries—for example, the U.S. government pays farmers to improve their lands by growing certain types of grasses. The PiK program (see Chapter 10) is one approach to consider.

Small-scale, Mutual-help Projects

The best and most effective projects are small-scale, mutual-help ones. Organization and monitoring are easier, and people usually take greater pride in the work. Most importantly, they can provide the basis for broader community-development efforts.

Normally, these activities are organized around small groups that live on adjacent sites. The type of activity usually determines the number of people who are mobilized. The only criterion is that everyone involved has to benefit directly from the project.

Community Projects

Projects that benefit the community are easy to identify: schools and public-health clinics readily come to mind. In a counterfamine program, however, it is important to remember that the activities selected should have an impact on food production—projects of general or longer-term benefit can wait.

Where it is desirable to avoid helping individuals or appearing to single out a specific group and where general income generation is important, public-works projects can be an appropriate choice.

Irrigation

Irrigation is an important method for reducing the subsistence farmers' vulnerability to drought. Even minor amounts of irrigation can make a significant difference in the perennial viability of crops. Wherever feasible, irrigation works should receive the highest priority.

Activities in this category include digging wells, irrigation canals, and localized channels and building water-lifting devices.

When organizing an irrigation project, those people who will directly benefit should be mobilized.

Land Improvements

The following activities can be used to improve farmland:

Erosion Control. The most common form of erosion control is contouring. Simple technologies, such as A-frames for determining contours (see Figure 8–1), have been developed that can be easily taught. Other measures that can be considered are planting windbreaks, constructing devices to capture and retain soil moisture, terracing hillsides, installing wells, improving existing ones, and improving irrigation and drainage.

Figure 8–1

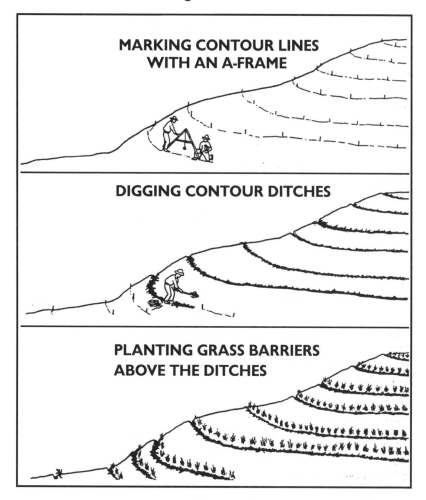

MARKING CONTOUR LINES WITH AN A-FRAME

DIGGING CONTOUR DITCHES

PLANTING GRASS BARRIERS ABOVE THE DITCHES

Terraces. Constructing terraces in mountainous areas serves several purposes. First, the terraces increase the amount of surface area available for farming. At the same time, the increased area provides a better surface for capturing and retaining rain without the erosion that usually accompanies cultivated hillsides. Terracing is labor intensive and therefore ideal for both local and area-wide projects. The design of the terraces must be carefully evaluated, however. If they are too small, they will have little effect.

Land-fertility Improvements. A number of activities can be encouraged that will improve the fertility of the land. These include:

- Rotational grazing of cattle or sheep
- Growing vegetative cover such as grasses, vetch (leafy, climbing or trailing plants that belong to the legume family), et cetera, on the land
- Alternative cropping
- Green manuring

In situations where there is not enough time to organize agricultural-rehabilitation projects before the next planting season begins, it may be necessary to pay farmers some form of income even though they are not working the land. It may even be desirable to give the land a rest to improve productivity the following season. In this case, do what agricultural ministries do in the industrialized countries: pay farmers to leave the land fallow or to carry out land improvements. Payments should be proportionate to the amount of income they would normally earn from the land they cultivate.

On-farm Grain Storage. Projects that build better storage bins and silos can immediately reduce farmers' losses. Such projects can be combined with community grain-bank programs that reduce famine vulnerability.

Fodder Harvesting. A serious effect of both droughts and floods is the loss of fodder available for large animals. In cases where crops sprouted but failed to mature, it is often possible to salvage the emergent grains for the animals to eat. For example, following a flood in Bangladesh, one agency financed a program to buy stalks from farmers to donate or sell as low-cost fodder for livestock. By brokering the tailings, the program provided income for a large number of farmers and helped others maintain their animals. In areas where there was little immediate need for the fodder, the agency erected some mobile silos and stored it until there was a demand some months later.

Counterdesertification Measures. There are a number of actions that can be taken to counter drought conditions and, in some cases, the spread of desert environments. They include:

- *Tree Planting.* One of the easiest ways to fight desertification is for farmers to plant trees around their fields and homes. Each tree encourages the growth of a related microecosystem and provides a small deterrent to wind-driven dust, sand, and water erosion.
- *Construction of Windbreaks.* Planting sturdy shrubs and trees as windbreaks between fields can help slow wind speeds. The

windbreaks reduce erosion and preserve valuable topsoils. They also can help regenerate grass cover and ultimately increase soil moisture.

- *Construction of Earthen or Stone Wind Barriers.* Wind barriers are small walls no more than a meter high that are placed at right angles to the prevailing wind. As wind blows against the barriers and is deflected upward, moisture is released, increasing the humidity around the barrier. Minute condensation forms and drops to the ground. Eventually, small green patches will begin to take root, and they can become quite large. They can often help replenish groundwater as well as provide small green spaces to protect against desert encroachment. (See Figure 8–2.)

- *Green Barriers.* Green belts can be created using green basins, a technique developed in Australia. A series of closely spaced, circular basins are made by plowing slight depressions or making circular banks in fields. These basins trap wind-blown seeds, which are nourished by moisture that is also trapped. When any amount of rain falls, small, temporary ponds form in the depression. The embankments or depressions also protect the seeds from dust storms. In Australia, green belts several kilometers wide and hundreds of kilometers long are often built as a line of defense, much like a firebreak, to prevent further encroachment of the desert. (See Figure 8–3.)

- *Sand Fences.* In areas where desertification is pronounced, sand fences can help reduce losses from sand piling. Eventually, however, the fences must be accompanied by larger, area-wide counterdesertification measures.

- *Water-supply Projects.* Provision of drinking water for humans as well as livestock is an important activity during most famines. The most common projects are:

  - *Digging Wells or Improving Existing Ones.* Digging or improving shallow open wells is an ideal project if increasing the draw on the aquifer will not deplete it. Well projects can be designed to benefit both small and large communities and can employ large numbers of workers. Digging a well, however, should be done only after the situation is studied. In arid-land agri-systems, wells attract herders and herd animals. This presents a new set of ecological and socioeconomic pressures for the areas and population surrounding the well.

  - *Dams.* Even in the worst droughts, some amount of rain usually falls. Often the water is lost, because it drains off

Figure 8-2

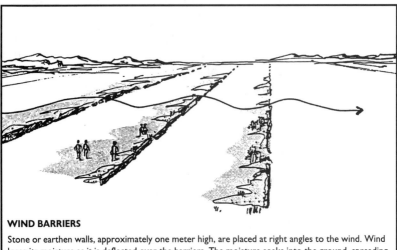

WIND BARRIERS

Stone or earthen walls, approximately one meter high, are placed at right angles to the wind. Wind loses its moisture as it is deflected over the barriers. The moisture soaks into the ground, spreading green growth. Soil stabilizes and more water is trapped.

before it can be trapped and stored. Therefore, an important water resource development strategy is the construction of *retention dams* at intervals across streambeds to trap flash-flood waters.

A variation of this approach is the *diversion dam*, which directs the water into channels leading to nearby depressions that can store a larger amount of water than the riverbed. (See Figure 8–4.) It may be possible in some cases to divert floodwaters directly into irrigation systems.

Subsurface dams are used to trap water in the sandy riverbeds of a dry stream, if the speed of the flash flood is likely to destroy a normal earthen retention dam. A trench is dug across the streambed down to a layer of impervious clay. The trench is then filled and packed with clay to form an underground dam. When flash floods occur, a portion of the water will be trapped in the sand behind the dam. Because the water is trapped in the sand, evaporation will be reduced. Small wells can then be dug by hand to reach the water. (See Figure 8–5.)

- *Construction of Haouris.* Haouris are man-made depressions dug in areas where highly expansive soils contract and seal when dampened. This prevents seepage. Haouris

Figure 8-3

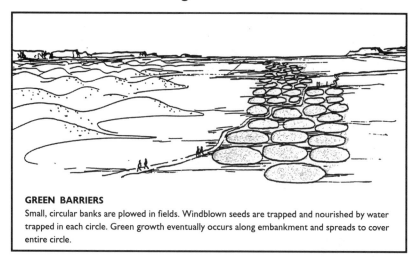

GREEN BARRIERS

Small, circular banks are plowed in fields. Windblown seeds are trapped and nourished by water trapped in each circle. Green growth eventually occurs along embankment and spreads to cover entire circle.

Figure 8-4

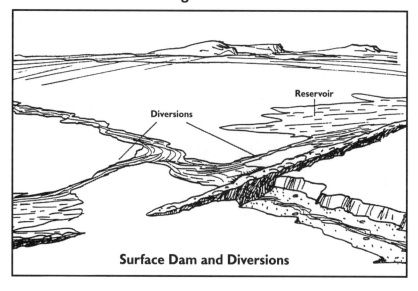

Surface Dam and Diversions

are often made in the arid savanna lands of Africa and in various locations in the Asian subcontinent. They are an excellent project for areas with large numbers of pastoralists.

Haouris can be filled with sand to reduce evaporation.

Figure 8–5

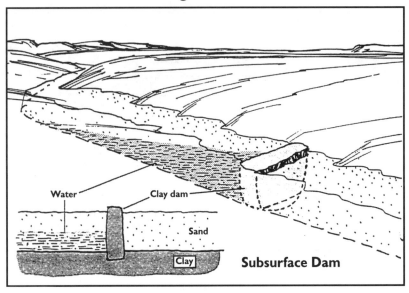

Water — Clay dam —

Sand

Clay

Subsurface Dam

The haouri is first enlarged, then filled with sand or gravel. Since sand is relatively porous, the amount of space it takes up is negligible compared to the water it saves from evaporation. In areas where desertification is advanced, people use the sand that builds up as the desert encroaches.

- *Recharging the Aquifer.* In cases where shallow aquifers are depleted, catchments can be built to trap surface water and permit it to seep quickly into the water-carrying strata. A number of methods can be used. The appropriate approach depends on the soils and the depth of the aquifer.

9 | *Emergency Response*

Introduction

Emergency response is the term used to describe the steps that need to be taken to respond to a fully developed famine.

The initial response is similar to the opening moves of a chess game. It is dictated as much by what is unknown about the situation as by what is known. In a chess game, no matter what the players' eventual strategy, pawns must be moved to create openings and flexibility for the capital pieces. Likewise, in an emergency, certain moves must be made and certain systems must be established before other options can be brought into play: lives cannot be saved unless certain interrelated measures are taken immediately. For example, diseases cannot be controlled unless an adequate food supply can be found. Food will have a reduced effect on people unless diarrhea is controlled. Diarrhea cannot be prevented unless an adequate supply of clean water exists. Clean water depends on adequate sanitation and good hygiene practices.

Emergency response should begin as soon as it becomes clear that counterfamine measures cannot prevent or contain a continued decline in people's nutritional status. At the same time, an assessment of the situation should be conducted (see Chapter 12). The information is then used to further elaborate the plans. Initial response should follow a prescribed pattern and continue until on-site assessments prove beyond a doubt that a specific set of interventions is not required. These actions should always be taken until accurate information is developed that indicates other measures should be employed.

Each of the main actions is complementary to and supports the others. One strategy alone usually will not solve a particular problem; a concerted attack involving several approaches is usually necessary. Furthermore, one program can rarely accomplish its goals unless it is supported by programs in other sectors. For example, death rates from diarrhea cannot be brought under control solely by providing clean

Figure 9-1

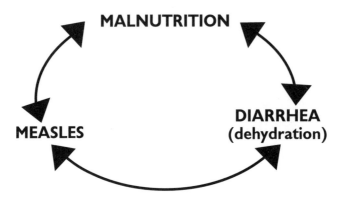

water; ORT (see Chapter 2) plus sanitation and good personal-hygiene practices are also important.

Epidemiological Considerations

Research has shown the primary causes of death in a famine are malnutrition, measles, and diarrhea. Each affects the others. A severely malnourished child will not survive a case of measles. Severe diarrhea can quickly dehydrate and kill a malnourished person or someone with measles. To save lives, these three killers must be brought under control.

The interrelationship of the three causes of mortality is depicted theoretically in Figure 9–1.

Primary Responses

The priorities in the initial phase of the emergency are those that address the major killers. These actions include supplying food, immunizing people, and controlling diarrhea through the provision of clean water, sanitation, hygiene, and oral rehydration.

These actions are the foundations of an initial-response doctrine. Each of these responses—food, immunization, and diarrhea control—requires a distinct set of activities.

Food Supply

Adequate supplies of food are required to ensure famine victims recover and maintain a good nutritional condition. This includes providing a general ration and, in some situations, supplementary food for special groups.

- *General Ration.* This is the ration designed to provide families with their basic food needs. Of all food supplied in emergencies, the general ration is the most important. If it is possible to supply enough food so that the general ration can be maintained without interruption, the vast majority of families can recover and survive on this food alone.

  The general ration is composed of a mix of foods—known as the *food basket*—designed to provide sufficient calories as well as protein, vitamins, and minerals. The primary requirements are:

  - Grain, oil, and minimum caloric content of 2,250–2,500 calories per day[1]

  - A source of protein

  - A mix of vitamins (especially A), minerals, and other nutrients to ensure healthy development of children

  The key to a successful general ration during the initial emergency is to supply enough food for people to survive without relying on supplementary sources. Usually, a general ration is based on giving every member of the family, even children, enough food to meet the needs of an adult. This permits families to apportion food according to nutritional needs and provides a small buffer against shortages and spoilage within the family's supply.

  The amount of food provided is determined by its caloric content—the lower the number of calories in a food, the greater the amount of food required. Most relief agencies calculate the amount needed on the basis of an average worker's nutrition requirements and adjust for interfamily distributions.

  Rations can be distributed at regular intervals to build confidence in the food supply and reduce hoarding. If relief camps have been set up, distributions should be made approximately every four to ten days. This reduces the likelihood that malnourished people who overconsume will not have enough food between the time they run out and the next distribution. Longer intervals will result in higher mortality.

  Unless an adequate registration program is developed and instituted immediately, major problems in food distribution will occur quickly.

- *Supplementary Feeding.* Supplementary feeding is a food-distribution program targeted for those who are malnourished or have special nutritional needs. A supplementary-feeding program should be undertaken:

- When malnutrition is high (more than 10 percent of those under five years)

- When there is evidence that families are not distributing food equitably among all family members and the problem cannot be corrected by other means such as changing the mix of foods distributed

- When the general ration is less than 1,900 calories for any reason

There are two ways to carry out supplementary-feeding programs. One is to supply special supplementary foods to the target populations, usually women and children under five. The other is to set up feeding centers where people come daily to receive prepared meals and consume them on the spot. Of the two programs, the latter is usually the most effective in the advanced stages of an emergency. However, it is only as effective as the efforts made by the staff to identify those most in need and to enroll them in the program and monitor attendance.

Weighing and measuring children to ensure they are gaining weight is important. Normally, middle upper-arm circumference measurements (called MUAC in the disaster-management world) are used for rapid community surveys to qualify children for supplementary feeding. Once they are enrolled, children are measured using weight-for-height standards.

If the program is being carried out via feeding centers, all children should be immunized against the primary childhood diseases (measles, et cetera) when they are enrolled. The minimum immunization necessary is measles.

In the initial stages of an emergency, the routine monitoring carried on as part of the program may be the best way to determine the population's other health and nutritional problems. By monitoring diarrhea in children and noting where people live, it is usually possible to identify impure sources of water. By noting women or children who do not gain weight despite supplementary feeding, problems can often be detected within the general ration or in the way food is distributed within the family.

The key to a successful supplementary-feeding program is outreach. Health workers must go into the community, identify women and children who require supplementary feeding, and ensure they are enrolled in the program and regularly receive supplementary food. Without an outreach effort, supplementary feeding will have only minimal impact.

- *Therapeutic (Intensive) Feeding.* Therapeutic feeding is an intensive, round-the-clock feeding program usually carried out under the supervision of health workers. In recent years, therapeutic-feeding programs have attracted much criticism from epidemiologists who note that few children survive despite the best efforts of medical staff. Therapeutic feeding requires special facilities, which are usually attached to an outpatient dispensary or hospital, and a skilled staff to monitor the feeding effort.

  As a general rule, therapeutic-feeding programs can be given a low priority in relation to other food and nutrition efforts. They should be established only after supplementary feeding is under way. In an emergency, the goal is to save as many people as possible, and efforts must be focused on keeping people from deteriorating to a point where radical interventions such as therapeutic feeding are necessary.

- *Indirect Food Supply.* Throughout the emergency, relief agencies should develop and expand indirect ways of increasing food supplies in and adjacent to the famine zone. These can include income-support projects, cash-for-work and food-for-work programs, and other indirect approaches. After the emergency has abated, direct food-aid programs should be phased out and indirect food programs should be expanded as a means of building food security.

  Food aid can only relieve food needs. It cannot eliminate the causes of famine. Furthermore, unchecked food aid can have adverse consequences, delaying agricultural recovery and creating dependencies on it. Therefore, a balanced famine-fighting strategy needs to be developed that includes not only food but also counterfamine strategies that aid in agricultural recovery and development assistance.

Immunization

Vaccinations to prevent communicable diseases, especially measles, are the second component of emergency response. To be successful, a vaccination program requires:

- Surveillance and detection of communicable diseases
- Vaccines
- A cold chain to ensure vaccines are not damaged or lose their strength from the point of origin to the time of injection
- Effective promotion, mobilization, and coverage of the population

In recent years, major efforts have been made to create adequate supplies of vaccines in all third-world countries. The Expanded Program of Immunization (EPI) spearheaded by the United Nations Children's Fund (UNICEF) and the UN's World Health Organization (WHO) has resulted in building national stockpiles of many of the most important vaccines used in emergencies, greatly reducing response times. By borrowing from EPI warehouses, there is no reason effective immunization campaigns cannot be carried out from the start of most emergencies.

A vital component is maintaining a continuous cold chain from the EPI warehouse to the recipient's arm. A cold chain requires the use of specially designed cold boxes—dedicated exclusively for holding vaccines—for transferring vaccines, refrigeration equipment, and adequate stores of fuel for the refrigerators at the immunization centers.

Diarrhea Control

Diarrhea control consists of both preventative and curative activities. Preventative actions focus on the relation between clean water, sanitation, and hygiene—known as the *hygiene loop*, illustrated below in Figure 9–2. Anywhere contamination occurs within this loop, diarrhea will result.

Curative actions focus on oral rehydration therapy, a simple solution of sugar, salt, baking soda, potassium chloride, and water that helps restore the body's electrolyte balance and treats dehydration. In the long term, it is more effective than most costly antidiarrheal medicines.

Use of ORT (oral rehydration therapy), or oral rehydration solution (ORS) as it is sometimes called, is becoming more widespread each year. In fact, in some countries, the packets are so commonplace, they are used for curing hangovers. (See Chapter 2.)

There are numerous sources for ORS packets. They are usually included in the standard medical kits provided by UNHCR, WHO, UNICEF, and many NGOs. Large stores of ORS packets are often on hand at the EPI warehouses, and they are commercially available in a growing number of countries. Where supplies are inadequate, it is possible to make the solution from the basic ingredients. The formula is below.

ORAL-REHYDRATION SOLUTION

Sodium chloride (table salt)	3.5 grams
Sodium bicarbonate (baking soda)	2.5 grams
Potassium chloride	1.5 grams
Glucose (sugar)	20.0 grams

The solution is mixed with one liter of clean water.

Figure 9-2

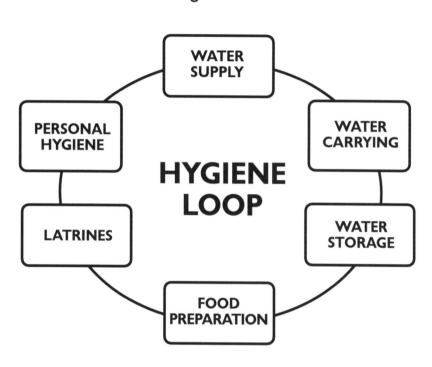

Notes

1. In most guides to relief operations, the recommended average emergency ration is 1,900 calories. Food, however, is more than a dietary need. The poor see it as a source of income. A starving family will often sell a portion of the food it receives to meet other needs such as income for travel or tools to increase productivity or supplement employment. This is frequently—and consciously—done at the nutritional expense of certain children in the family. In some societies, for example, male children are favored nutritionally. If the basis for planning the ration does not consider this factor and adjust the allocation upward, some members of the family will not have enough to eat to survive.

10 | *Food-relief Programs*

Introduction

There are a number of ways to ensure people get the food they need during famines. These methods can be categorized as either direct or indirect. No one means will meet all the people's needs at the same time. Thus, planners can consider using a mix of programs in various phases of the famine. Based on Cutler's model, Figure 10–1 depicts a typical famine cycle and shows how different approaches might be applied at different phases to improve the targeting of food aid and, at the same time, promote agricultural recovery.

There are many alternatives to direct food distribution during times of famine or conflict. They include:

- Market interventions, including:
  - Internal-purchase programs
  - Direct sale of food to local vendors at subsidized rates, that is, monetization of food aid
  - Livestock interventions
- Income-support programs such as cash for work
- Food-for-work programs (FFW)
- Food-stamp or food-coupon programs
- Payment-in-Kind programs

If these programs are properly planned, they are less stressful to families than handouts. Alternatives can also infuse food into an area in ways that often consider events that contributed to the famine. These alternatives can stabilize food prices and support normal income generation, reducing social stress and dependency that often come with food handouts. Some of these programs were outlined in Chapter 7. Here they are reviewed in more detail and with special reference to their use in the later stages of a famine.

Figure 10-1

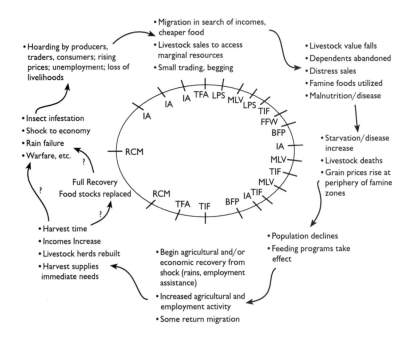

IA—Income assistance/support

TFA—Targeted food aid

MLV—Monetization to local vendors

FFW—Food-for-work programs

LPS—Livestock price support

BFP—Broad-based feeding programs

TIF—Targeted intensive feeding for vulnerable

RCM—Resource conservation measure/groups

Monetization

Monetization is the sale of donated relief food to generate currency for other purposes. For many years, monetization was the practice of giving food to governments, which would then sell it and use the proceeds to assist development projects, balance of payments, or administrative needs. Although the monetization of relief food is still hampered by regulations and attitudes that keep it from being used more effectively in counterfamine measures, relief professionals are beginning to understand its value in small-scale food-relief and market-intervention programs.

Direct Monetization

Direct monetization is an approach used to revitalize village grain markets. Supplies of grain are procured and delivered to target villages, where they are sold at subsidized prices directly to small retail vendors in the market. The selling price should be an amount equivalent to the normal wholesale price. Sales to each vendor should be limited, and purchasers should agree to sell their grains within a certain price range, roughly equivalent to the normal (or previous season's) retail-sales price, adjusted for inflation. The retail market should be monitored to ensure vendors sell the grain within the agreed limits. Any vendor selling above that level or selling to wholesale merchants would be disqualified from subsequent sales.

Proceeds from the sale can go into a village fund to be used for cash-for-work projects. Families that cannot afford to buy grain at the depressed price would be eligible to apply for employment in the cash-for-work projects. The village council or elders would select projects, which would be monitored by NGOs working in the area.

Indirect Monetization Programs

Monetization can be used as a strategy to reach people in areas that are insecure and inaccessible to relief agencies. Merchants and others who remain in the area are often willing to buy food and transport it to the region. Many private merchants from Eritrea bought food in Sudan and took it back into the besieged territory throughout the civil war there. Sometimes they would carry the grain by lorry, but often they would take it in by camel or donkey. Other examples where merchants managed to get food into areas that relief agencies found difficult or impossible to reach include Afghanistan, Sri Lanka, Somalia, and the famous land-bridge operation in Cambodia. The merchants are often able to negotiate deals with the warring parties that allow them to cross the lines, and larger merchants can usually organize protection for shipments. Smaller village traders who use pack animals frequently reach areas off the main roads and travel at night, so they avoid bandits and irregular forces.

Food sold in an indirect monetization program will cost more in the retail markets because of the wholesale traders' added costs. However, merchants are mindful of what prices the market can bear and will usually recognize there is more profit in volume sales than in limited, high-price trade. Usually, the prices for the first deliveries are relatively high, but as the wealthier people's food needs are satisfied and deliveries continue, the price begins to drop. Unfortunately, this means those who need food most, the poorest individuals and people who are out of cash, usually have to wait the longest for food. In Afghanistan, agencies

tried to offset this by working with the merchants to get them to allo-
cate a portion of food to the poorest, but this proved difficult to monitor.
In Somalia in 1992–93, funds from monetization efforts were used for
cash-for-work programs targeted to the most needy. This program attracted merchants, who delivered food and thus expanded markets.
When more expensive grain was delivered, people who had money
bought this food, resulting in a drop in price for other grains such as
sorghum, which the lower classes tended to buy.

Indirect monetization may not be the best approach, but it can reduce levels of theft and danger to NGO personnel as well as the costs of
delivering relief food. It also supports traditional commercial activities
that, in turn, can create employment, feed local economies, and redirect
energy from conflict to commerce. In some cases, indirect monetization
is the only way to deliver food where it is needed.

Internal-purchase Programs

In many situations, the purchase and distribution of internally available food reserves is a viable alternative to imported food aid. In most
conflicts and famines, the amount of food available is significantly greater
than outsiders realize, and cereals, pulses, and livestock are often ob-
tainable. Since famines are usually the result of market disturbances
and conflicts that disrupt normal marketing, food is often trapped in
pockets where it cannot be sold or transported as usual. In an internal-
purchase program, a relief agency locates sources of supply, imports
local currency to buy food, and then purchases and redistributes it,
either by selling it at lower prices or giving it to relief agencies or committees in the famine or conflict zone to distribute through selective
feeding or targeted food programs.

Internal purchase has many advantages. It is faster than importing
food, is less costly, and can usually be managed by a few people working with local merchants and traders. Once merchants release food they
are hoarding, others will also start to sell, especially if the agency is
reselling food to local vendors at low prices. Internal purchase's primary advantage is helping to reactivate the normal market system.

Food obtained through internal-purchase operations is often more
compatible with local tastes than imported foods. When food is sold,
proceeds can be used to buy more food or to support cash-for-work
projects that give the poorest people a chance to earn money.

While internal-food supplies are often more effective than exter-
nal-food aid, one must ensure that buying and distributing it does not
significantly disrupt the local economy. Since famines shift geographically, it is important to carefully analyze food availability before
purchasing internally. For example, villages outside the famine zone

may produce a surplus. However, if villages next to them are producing at marginal or subsistence levels, those villagers may depend on the surplus for their own protection. Thus, careful analysis is required before initiating an internal-purchase program.

Cash-for-work Programs

A cash-for-work program, when properly organized, is the easiest way of providing people with money to buy food on a widespread basis. Programs are relatively easy to plan and execute, and monitoring is simple. The only major concern is the types of projects selected: they must not take people away from normal agricultural activities and should be designed to improve both near- and long-term agricultural prospects.

In comparison with food-for-work programs, which are generally more popular with relief agencies, cash for work is less disruptive of the local economy. The program is easier to administer—there are no commodity logistics to manage—and the projects are easier to terminate and to move from one area to another, as needs dictate.

Cash for work also can infuse much-needed money into economies depleted of cash resources by drought and famine. In some cases, this can stimulate local economic recovery.

Culturally, cash for work is not an alien concept. People normally work for wages. Therefore, the program is the best way to help maintain people's dignity, since it removes the stigma of working on a relief program and gives people a choice about how they use the money.

Critics of cash for work claim people do not spend all their money on food. The purpose of the program is to fight famine, they say, and food is what is needed. This criticism can also be leveled at food-for-work programs: FFW food can be sold, and the family can use the money to buy whatever it needs. In reality, uses of cash vary from culture to culture. When this issue arises, it tends to be a complicated cultural concern that a counterfamine program is not designed to address. Critics also point out that money can make it more profitable for people to work for cash than to work in the fields, if projects pay more than farming. Also, in a country like Ethiopia, where restrictions controlled the movement of food between agricultural areas and there were no natural market forces to move surpluses to food-deficit areas, there may not be enough food to buy in these regions. This could push up prices in local markets and lower the buying power of the cash received.

Inexperienced relief managers often set cash-for-work program wages at artificially high rates to provide immediate income for the participants. While this is a well-meaning act, it raises the expectations of wage earners, attracts farmers away from their farms, and draws more affluent workers from town who may use influence to replace needier workmen on the cash-for-work payroll.

Cash-for-work projects should:

- Be short term

- Be paid on a piecework basis

- Include women as workers

- Use a screening process to determine who is eligible

- Keep wages at modest levels

Projects may be carried out any time in the planting cycle, but if off-farm projects are planned during peak cultivation or harvest periods, allowances for part-time work must be made so that people can work their lands at these critical times.

Cash-for-work programs can be used as exit programs in areas where food aid is being phased out. This will inject much-needed capital into the local economy and help continue both agricultural and economic recovery.

Food-for-work Programs

Typically, FFW projects pay people with food for working on public-works or community-development projects. Ideally, food-for-work programs are used to improve the land or make improvements that will aid agriculture, such as terracing, building water catchments, erosion-control measures, and irrigation. On a larger basis, FFW may be used for community improvements such as building or upgrading farm-to-market roads.

Food-for-work proponents maintain the program is less likely to create dependencies than direct food aid and is more developmental than direct handouts. Food for work also accomplishes multiple objectives: getting food into the hands of those most in need and carrying out projects and improvements that benefit everyone. Thus, both individuals and communities are served.

Projects are not difficult to organize, though paying in food means a food-logistics-and-warehouse system must be set up to transport and store food prior to distribution. The only difference logistically between FFW and a direct-distribution program is that final distribution is easier in FFW and does not require the same degree of monitoring.

However, food for work has critics, who point out that, unless properly planned, FFW often takes on a life of its own. As more food enters the community, some will inevitably be sold on the local market to buy things people need other than food. Food is normally sold below market price, which depresses the amount farmers can get for food they have been able to produce—thus that group is added to the overall caseload. As prices for agricultural products decline, it quickly pays more to work for food than to grow crops. Gradually, production drops, causing more hunger and forcing more people to go to work for food. More food is needed to meet the need, and soon a vicious cycle is established. Critics have noted that dry-ration distribution is often easier to stop than food-for-work programs.

The objective of any feeding program is to feed people most at risk, and in famines, those most at risk are children. Critics of FFW point out that it is difficult to establish a correlation between food-for-work programs and nutritional improvement. Able-bodied men usually participate in food-for-work programs, and because they are undertaking strenuous work, they take a larger portion of food. To compensate, more food may have to be given out. This means that more food will be necessary. In a situation where food resources are scarce, it may be more expeditious to continue dry-ration distribution than to phase into a more resource-consuming program that can discourage agricultural production.

Food for work is normally used:

- As a counterfamine measure
- As a complementary approach to increasing food in a community during a famine emergency
- As a means of increasing food security at the periphery of the famine zone to contain the spread of famine

Food for work is most often compared to cash for work, with an increasing number of advocates choosing the latter. In reality, both types of projects can be appropriate under certain circumstances, if properly planned and carried out. In reality, Western countries produce food surpluses, not cash. In the past, humanitarian organizations were more likely to obtain food for distribution. Consequently, they were more likely to carry out food-for-work programs than cash for work. In recent years, with agricultural subsidies declining as well as foreign aid budgets, food is not necessarily more available than cash for famine response. Such organizations should establish criteria for the formulation of these projects that will make the program as nondisruptive as possible and explore options that could provide an alternative food-distribution mechanism.

Critics of both approaches believe food-for-work projects are often make-work activities, and if they are not needed, they can consume valuable resources. Unless well planned, the projects can also lure large numbers of people who are attracted by good wages—known as a *labor pole*. These labor poles draw farmers away from food production, prolonging the famine. Such projects require detailed study and planning, but people without proper training and skill often set them up.

Therefore, the programs may not be environmentally sound and can have an adverse effect on local ecologies and agriculture.

Food-for-work programs should be designed to provide short-term work only. To ensure this happens, projects should be small-scale activities that can be completed in a short period. Projects such as road construction that take months or years to complete or that could be intentionally prolonged by workers or program administrators should be avoided.

Projects should be conducted between planting and harvest periods, begin three months after the normal harvest and continue until the next planting season, or allow for simultaneous work and cultivation. If projects are carried out during the planting season, they could reduce the amount of food being cultivated. If run during the harvest season or immediately thereafter, the project food could depress local prices, because they put more food on the market. All programs should have a predetermined and widely advertised end date.

An appropriate mix of projects can be planned for the same area. Not all projects should be targeted at the agricultural sector, but they should include works that will improve living conditions in the famine zones.

Payment for work should be according to production rather than a daily wage, that is, piecework. When farmers are the primary target group, the work should be on a part-time basis only, perhaps two or three days per week, unless the agricultural season is a fallow one, to permit farmers to work their fields.

In areas where agricultural recovery is taking place, food for work should be a preliminary step to phasing out food aid. The phase-out should occur when nutritional levels have stabilized and remained high for three months or longer. Effective screening procedures can be established to ensure men working in food-for-work programs represent the neediest households and those with a high percentage of vulnerable individuals.

To ensure vulnerable groups receive food, food-for-work projects should be developed for women.

Food-store-and-coupon Approach

A variation on food for work is the *food-store-and-coupon program*. This program has been used with variations in several countries with significant success. A number of experts have suggested this approach can help address problems associated with both food-for-work and cash-for-work programs.

Under the program, income-generating projects similar to those established for food-for-work programs are organized. However, the workers are paid in *coupons* that can be redeemed only at a special relief store set up in each community. These stores stock food, but also carry other supplies such as health-care items, charcoal, household utensils, and personal articles that can contribute to health and hygiene such as soap and toothpaste. In addition, a limited number of personal luxury items may also be sold at the store. Cash or a combination of cash and coupons can be used to purchase these items.

Under this approach, the rationale goes, people will buy only what they need. This serves as a natural regulator of the amount of food coming into the community. Also, people will have the ability to buy those things they would otherwise obtain by selling food. Therefore, food provided by the relief program will not be as likely to end up in the local market competing with food produced by local farmers.

If participating agencies procure the luxury items from the local market, local shopkeepers will also benefit. The amount of input from the agencies should be minimal, and by having a greater range of items at the food store, the program should be popular and produce incentives to work. Finally, the range of foods provided at the coupon store can include those that are specially targeted for vulnerable groups, theoretically ensuring that a greater number of people most in need of calorie and nutritional inputs will receive them. With items in the store being controlled by relief agencies, it would be possible to ensure that the workers take home primarily food, although nothing prevents the commodities from the store from being sold for cash.

Proponents of the coupon-store programs also point out it is easy to establish nutrition-monitoring activities in conjunction with and physically adjacent to the relief store. Open hours can be established and redemption days can be printed on the coupons.

The criteria for the coupon-food-store program are the same as those for food-for-work projects. However, since the food-store concept is less likely to put surplus food into the market, the program may be carried out on a year-round basis.

Payment-in-Kind Programs

PiK programs are designed to help support local farmers and to maintain or reconstruct the normal food-marketing system. Under this approach, farmers are paid in grains to improve their land with counterdrought or counterdesertification measures such as contouring, terracing, or planting windbreaks and for participating in community-development projects such as water-harvesting measures for a specified period. Instead of receiving wages, farmers are given an amount of food that is equivalent to the amount of grain they would have produced had conditions been normal. If their harvest has totally failed, they receive the full amount. They obtain the balance, if they harvest a percentage of their normal yield.

Farmers are usually paid in unmilled grains. They can sell the grains at whatever price they can negotiate from their normal buyers. In this way, all people and institutions normally engaged in the marketing system can carry on as if the drought had not occurred. The negative impact of drought on the market system can thus be substantially reduced.

Advocates point out that PiK provides an excellent means of informally controlling prices in local markets. This is done by adjusting the percentages of food provided according to normal yields. By providing a greater percentage, prices should move downward; by providing less, prices would move upward.

PiK is designed to be used in those areas that are beginning to experience drought conditions or where some agricultural recovery has been possible in the aftermath of widespread crop failures. It should not be used in an area where almost total crop failure occurs for more than one year.

Proponents of PiK maintain the program is the least disruptive to the local-market system. They also point out that having additional grains will enable farmers producing limited amounts of locally acclimatized grains to reserve an adequate portion of their yield for seeds for the following season. This reduces the amount of seed that relief agencies or the government need to provide.

Because the food system remains intact, proponents point out, the overall agro-economy can benefit others, not just farmers. Some proponents also estimate that management requirements for PiK are less than those for other programs, since food is being handled through the normal market system and not through an artificial distribution system. Food does not need to be delivered to each farmer but can be taken to the granaries and allocated to farmers when their harvest is brought in for sale. In Ethiopia, PiK programs may have stabilized grain markets in areas that were marginally affected by drought and countered famine in isolated food-deficit areas. PiK could also be used in those areas where food is growing, but not in sufficient quantities.

PiK programs should be targeted for areas where:

- Famine conditions do not currently exist, but food availability is decreasing
- Famine conditions exist, but food deficits are decreasing, and agricultural recovery is taking place
- Food deficits occur adjacent to acute famine areas
- Isolated pockets of food deficit are surrounded by areas of food sufficiency although not major surpluses

Fair-price Stores

The fair-price store is a popular way of providing indirect controls over food-market prices while making commodities available at reasonable prices to those most in need. This approach has been used in a number of countries, but it is most often associated with India, Bangladesh, and Sri Lanka. The concept grew out of the famine codes that were developed following the food crises in that region in the mid-nineteenth century.

Fair-price stores are places where staples are sold at normal prices. The objective is to stabilize prices in the market during times of scarcity by providing a nearby distributor who sells at a fair price. By charging less, the fair-price store forces others in the market to lower their prices or lose business.

The stores can operate in several ways. On the subcontinent, the governments ran the stores. In Haiti, cooperatives have run similar stores for their members. In Kenya, the government has sold grain at low prices to dealers in the village markets. The dealers, in turn, agree to resell the grain to the villagers at a fair price negotiated with the government. In

---

Principles for Employing Indirect Food Aid

The following principles can guide agencies in determining when to use and how to target alternative food-aid programs:

- Alternative food-aid strategies may be used when nutrition-based distribution systems are being employed for the larger community

- Alternative food programs should be used as the primary vehicle for transition from intensive to limited food aid

- Food aid should not be used to employ people to do work they would normally do without pay, such as improvements to their own land or traditional community labor

- Food-for-work programs should be carefully monitored to ensure people who need food receive first priority for jobs

- The food-for-work programs should be monitored to ensure the amount of food provided does not have a disruptive effect on agricultural activities such as planting and harvesting or on market prices. These programs also should not pull farmers away from food production.

several countries, NGOs have operated the stores, using grains they obtained as commodity aid from major donors.

In many cases, access to the fair-price stores is limited to registered beneficiaries who must present a ration card or other form of identification to purchase food. In several countries that use food stamps, anyone who qualifies for the stamps can shop at the stores. Several programs allow anyone access to the stores, but the amount they can purchase at one time is limited.

The primary advantage of the fair-price store is that it uses a familiar mechanism, with minimum disruption of the normal markets, to fight price gouging and ensure people access to food.

Direct Food-distribution Systems

There are many ways to distribute food during a famine, and there are many models and programs that have developed over years of practice that can be adapted for specific situations.

The choice of approach is usually dictated by:

- The severity of the famine
- The geographic location of people
- The degree of insecurity in the area of distribution
- Whether people are living in their villages or have moved to relief camps in search of food

Generally, direct programs distribute food directly to the famine victims, usually free of charge although sometimes a token payment or service may be encouraged.

Direct food-distribution systems can be divided into two categories: village and camp systems. During widespread famine, relief agencies are often involved in both.

There are major differences in the approach to village and camp distributions. Village systems are designed to help people remain in their homes and to continue living as normally as possible. This assumes people usually have access to other food sources; therefore, the system is *supplemental*. The agency attempts to put enough food into the community to meet all its nutritional needs and to allow natural adjustments to take place—in other words, to provide enough food so that people can sell or barter food for other services. Under this approach, however, food distribution should not be so great that farmers slow or cease agricultural production. Food distribution also should not adversely affect the prices farmers can get for food they harvest. At the same time, it is important for those who need food most to get adequate amounts so they will gradually improve nutritionally.

Village-distribution systems are the more difficult logistically and administratively to carry out, but the advantages of this program over camp-based systems far outweigh the inconveniences. People who remain in their communities can continue their lives. They will also be present when conditions in their area have improved enough to permit resumption of normal activities, and food production can be restored to its normal levels. Village systems are therefore more developmental than camp systems, which are better described as relief programs.

Camp systems are required when people leave their homes in search of food and congregate in relief camps or in highly dense settlements adjacent to cities. The program must assume that people, because they have left home, do not have access to other food sources and that relief agencies must meet the total food requirements of the victims. Even if the settlement or camp is adjacent to a major city, the program must assume, at least at first, that the displaced people do not have access to other food sources. Later, it may be possible to decrease the amount of relief if evidence indicates that people are able to obtain other sources of food.

The camp systems, however, can encourage a spiral of displacement. As people begin to believe they will find greater food security in a camp or city, farmers who are only marginally supplying adequate food for their families may decide they stand a better chance in a camp run by a foreign relief organization. This then becomes a self-fulfilling prophecy as farmers leave the farm, crops fail, and the donor community assumes control of their welfare.

When providing food in camps, an organization needs to hand out a balanced food basket. This means food that is distributed must meet all basic requirements for nutrition including calories, protein, vitamins, and minerals for members of a typical family.

Other major concerns in camp systems are:

- Providing food on a regular and timely basis
- Ensuring equitable interfamily distribution of food

People living in camps are usually more vulnerable than people who have been able to remain in their villages. Therefore, caution must be exercised in carrying out a free distribution program to ensure that it is equitable.

Village-distribution Systems

Two models can be used: *general-distribution systems* and *nutrition-based distribution systems*.

General-distribution Systems

In the general system, a relief agency takes food in bulk to the villages and distributes it to everyone equally on a regular basis. The ration is usually based on a fixed allocation (determined by caloric content) multiplied by the number of family members.

This approach has several advantages. First, it is the easiest to plan. Simply multiply the number of people by the food ration to get the total tonnage required. Second, the program is fairly simple to manage. Most of the emphasis is on logistics management rather than complicated nutrition monitoring. Third, since all the people are receiving food, a slight surplus will develop in each community, because the planning process counts all recipients as adults in need of food. Also many people are likely to surreptitiously register more than once. This surplus will eventually be stockpiled for future needs or bartered by the families for other needed goods and services. Since every member of the community is receiving food, questions of equity and intravillage distribution are minimized.

The disadvantages of the program, however, usually outweigh the advantages. First, the neediest people are not specifically targeted. Therefore, some of the most desperate may not receive as much food as they need because of diversions or inequitable interfamily distribution of food. Second, it is the most expensive program. Since everyone is receiving food regardless of need, more food and transportation is required than if only the neediest were being fed.

The biggest disadvantage is surplus food in the community, which could slow agricultural recovery. The surplus could undercut the prices farmers could get for the food they produce. That could harm farmers and small merchants and delay recovery.

Phasing out such a program may also be difficult and is often disruptive. Since everyone in the community is getting food, it is more difficult to spot those who need additional nutritional support. Reducing the program without targeting specific people could mean those not fully recovered would be harmed.

Finally, general food-distribution programs are difficult to adjust to meet the needs of those groups with special nutritional requirements.

Nutrition-based Distribution Systems

In nutrition-based systems, a parent, usually the mother, brings the thinnest child to a food-distribution center and receives a food allocation based on the needs of that child. Initially, everyone in the family receives a general ration. Later, the program is adjusted to meet the needs of only the malnourished.

The middle-upper-arm-circumference method of nutrition surveillance is normally used to determine whether a child should be enrolled in the program. This method tends to err on the side of caution. In other words, all those who are on the margins are likely to qualify for at least one month's food support. Once people are enrolled in the program, more accurate weight-for-height measurements will be used to monitor progress.

The advantages of the nutrition-based system clearly outweigh the disadvantages. First, it provides better targeting. Food gets directly to people most in need in each community. Second, the programs are easy to adjust. Because regular nutritional monitoring is carried out, people most in need receive food, and those who prove to be healthy can be discharged quickly. If food conditions in the community continue to deteriorate, more people can be easily enrolled and exact food needs can be calculated.

The per capita cost is less. Since food is targeted to actual needs, surpluses do not develop and transport can be tailored to meet those real needs.

Because food is going to those most in need, there is little adverse impact on the market. In most cases, consumption will equal distribution, and the normal system will not be affected either positively or negatively.

Nutrition-based systems provide a means of monitoring other factors or problems in the community, especially disease, and in extreme situations, death rates. For example, if the distributing agency monitors such factors as diarrhea, disease, and attendance at the distribution center and keeps records of participants by addresses or locations in the

---

Requirements for Establishing a General Village-distribution System

A nutritional assessment should first be done. Then:

1. Establish a logistics system and procure vehicles, fuel, and maintenance facilities.
2. Establish a registration system.
3. Designate distribution points in each community.
4. Establish a regular distribution schedule.
5. Establish a monitoring system with in-house checks linked to specific addresses in each community.

community, it is often possible to identify problems such as impure sources of water (detected by higher-than-normal diarrhea rates) and the prevalence of contagious diseases such as measles and other illnesses associated with malnutrition. It is also possible to monitor the geographic dimensions and spread of famine conditions.

Finally, it is easy to phase out the program when it is no longer needed. There is less impact on farmers, because food aid has been better fitted to needs.

The disadvantages of a nutrition-based system are few but are important to recognize. Nutrition-based distribution systems are more difficult and costly to administer, at least at first. However, monitoring permits administrators to discharge people when conditions have improved enough, so they can take care of their own food requirements. Planning for food needs is more complicated, because it has to be adjusted monthly. To receive the full benefits of the approach, more sophistication in operations is required. The distribution centers must be closely monitored and the data continually analyzed throughout the program. However, once the program is set up and in operation, these functions become routine and are not difficult.

More staff is required. Nutrition-based programs are usually carried out by a voluntary agency with specialized health personnel. Sometimes UNICEF or government health ministries may be involved, though this is rare.

Good record keeping is required not only for the program but also for each individual case. Without good records, it is impossible to make the adjustments that make this program cost effective.

Many critics of this approach are concerned that families may withhold food from one child, so they can remain in the program longer than is necessary. This behavior, referred to as the *starve-a-child syndrome*, is rare. If the agency does a series of spot checks to investigate intrafamily distribution of food, this syndrome can usually be quickly detected. If the behavior is widespread, the syndrome can be overcome by distributing food that only children have a taste for or that adults would not likely eat such as strained or blended foods like bulgur wheat or corn-soya milk, a common relief food used in supplementary-feeding programs for children. Other popular blended foods include wheat-soya blend, corn-soya blend, and UNIMIX, a special United Nations blend.

Common Problems in Village-distribution Systems

Experience has shown there are certain problems that tend to occur in village distribution programs. These are:

- *Multiple Registration*. This usually occurs when agencies unfamiliar with the community begin distribution. People quickly

---

Requirements for Establishing
a Nutrition-based Distribution System

A nutritional assessment should be conducted first. Then:

1. Establish a logistics system and procure vehicles, fuel, and maintenance facilities.

2. Establish a registration system based on:
   - Entry, using the middle-upper-arm-circumference measurement system
   - In-center monitoring using weight-for-height measurement systems

3. Establish distribution points with in-house screening areas (with weighing scales, height-for-weight charts, registration cards, et cetera).

4. Establish a distribution schedule that permits adequate time for each case.

5. Provide one nutritionist to monitor several distribution centers and to analyze the data being collected.

---

recognize they can give bogus information and register more than once.

To combat multiple registration, families need to be "fixed" to a geographic location for their food distribution. Spot checks should be carried out to be sure people are not cheating.

- *Inflated Numbers of Family Members.* People often try to exaggerate the number of children in their families if the agency does not enroll people after on-site inspections. This behavior can be corrected by doing spot checks after the families have been enrolled. But this is difficult, unless the checks are conducted at a time when the entire family is likely to be together, such as at night or during meals. Using people from the village to help enroll beneficiaries may be another way to reduce cheating, but local staff members may also cheat, because they are likely to be sympathetic to their neighbors.

- *Inflated Numbers of People in a Village.* This is often a problem when village leaders are put in charge of preparing the distribution lists for handing out food in their village. They may think they need to inflate the number to ensure people get adequate amounts of food. If village leaders are providing the relief lists, spot checks should be carried out to verify the number of people in families and the number of families in clans or villages.

- *Registration of People Who Are Not Eligible.* Often, people who are not eligible for food distribution will attempt to enroll to obtain food to sell or barter. To do this, they may borrow a child or other adults and create a bogus family to qualify them for enrollment. Detecting noneligibles is difficult, especially for an outside agency unfamiliar with the community. The best way to detect this behavior is through trusted local workers who verify the claims of each person or family.

- *Failure to Report Deaths of Family Members.* It is common for families to hide the death of a family member, so they can continue to receive that person's ration. Many relief agencies find themselves caught in an adversarial situation with their clients over this issue. Since mortality is the major indicator of the performance of a program, it is important this data is collected. As a general rule, agencies should make it clear that food rations will not be reduced simply because one or more children have died. The amount of oversupplied food in this case is minimal. Mortality information is far more valuable, and the additional food that a child would have brought in can be sold to help defray costs of burial, et cetera.

Camp-distribution Systems

When large numbers of people have congregated in camps or at the edge of cities in spontaneous settlements, it is usually necessary to distribute food to them directly. Indirect food systems are usually not used except to pay workers for camp operations.

In-camp distribution systems are usually divided into *wet feeding* and *dry feeding* (or dry-ration distribution). Wet feeding refers to the preparation of a cooked meal, while dry feeding refers to the distribution of food in bulk to families or groups of families, so they can prepare it themselves in their shelters.

Wet feeding is the least desirable food-distribution method, though it is sometimes necessary. It is most often used to feed new arrivals, small populations, specific groups who have special nutritional needs, or people too weak or otherwise incapable of food preparation. Wet-food distribution can also reduce schemes to collect and sell extra food. Since wet food must be consumed on the spot, it has no resale value.

Dry rations are the most common means of distributing food. They require less staff, and they enable people to carry on life-styles as near to normal as possible.

In most cases, dry rations should be all the food aid required. Special feeding programs should not be necessary if adequate supplies are available and if the basis for food distribution assumes adequate portions for all family members and provides enough food so people may barter or exchange food. In most cases, however, relief agencies cut the margins close. At least initially, distributions may be haphazard and periodic shortages may occur. In these cases, inequities in the food-distribution system may result as well as inequitable distributions among family members. When this happens, a supplementary-food distribution may be necessary. This may be done by providing a supplementary dry ration for vulnerable groups, by providing special infant foods that are not likely to be consumed by adults or older children, or, in extreme cases, by conducting a supplementary-feeding program where prepared meals are given to women and children who come to a special supplementary-feeding center.

Dry Ration-distribution Methods

The two most common methods for distributing foods in a dry-ration system are to individuals and to groups.

- *Individual Distributions.* In the individual system, each family is registered and issued a ration card. On specified days, one member of the family goes to the distribution point and, upon presentation of the ration card, collects the family's ration. Distributions are straightforward. As long as the distribution points are spread throughout the community, distribution can be done quickly and without too much trouble.

  If registration is thorough and well monitored, each family is certain to get its full ration. That is the primary advantage of the system. But the system requires a lot of staff, and there must be constant checking to make sure cheating is kept to a minimum. Furthermore, if the registration system is not adequate and is not address based, multiple registration is easy and accurate targeting is almost impossible.

- *Group Distributions.* In group distribution, food is delivered in bulk to a sector or community unit of a camp or to a section of a community and distributed in bulk to the group leaders from that area. The leaders then distribute food to people based on their assessment of needs.

  In recent years, this has become a popular distribution

method, especially where the recipients belong to the same village, tribe, clan, or extended family. Many sociologists argue this method helps keep family and cultural units together and assists in reinforcing the position of traditional leaders. Several critics, however, warn that traditional leaders may take an unfair portion for themselves as their prerogative. And some studies have indicated that where group systems are used, nutritional recovery of the severely malnourished is often delayed and mortality rates take longer to decline, usually because intergroup distribution is not equitable.

From an administrative point of view, group-distribution programs are fast and easy to monitor. Individual-registration systems are not necessary, although it is important for the agency to do verifications and spot checks to ensure the number of people claimed by the community leaders is accurate.

The primary disadvantage of group distributions is the difficulty in controlling the allocation of food. In addition, within the community, certain groups may not be receiving their fair share. As a general rule, group distributions should be avoided when:

- A strong caste system exists, and the society and its caste relations are generally intact

- The society has a practice of indentured servitude, slavery, or holding captives as laborers. In these situations, these groups will be denied food and high mortality will result.

- Hostile insurgent groups are in the camp and may use food as a means of controlling the population

- The system will make women vulnerable to sexual exploitation. When men control the system, withholding food for sexual favors is commonplace, particularly in camps where a number of widows or other single women exist without traditional protection mechanisms.

11 | *Famine Logistics*

Introduction

All famine interventions require logistical support. Conventional food-aid responses, many counterfamine programs, and all immunization efforts entail the movement of supplies and personnel from one point to another. Even market interventions require movement of food to a point where it can be sold to the merchants. Without an effective logistics system, no relief operation can achieve its objectives.

Logistics are not complicated, yet few organizations properly implement logistics operations. There are too few experienced or trained logisticians working in emergency operations. As a result, this key activity is often plagued with problems and costly delays.

Logistics for emergency-relief operations are different from most other types of logistics. The need for the speedy delivery of supplies is often complicated by ad hoc structures that draw personnel and equipment from several nonprofessional organizations. Because the procedures of the group are not standard, there is often some initial confusion that complicates operations and creates logjams. Unless these problems are addressed at the beginning, they can quickly multiply and further delay deliveries.

Definition

A good working definition of emergency logistics is:

The practical art of establishing lines of supply and providing commodities and the transport to move them.

The term *lines of supply* is important; logistics should be thought of as a linear system—a flow of supplies from point to point along a linear route. Another way to view logistics is as a system of supply, where items flow through the system in one direction and documents describing that flow return in the other direction. For example, commodities such as food move down the system, while requisitions and reports flow back to the system's managers at each control point.

The Importance of Logistics

Logistics is the lifeline of a relief operation. People depend on food and other supplies in the logistics system.

Logistics is often the most expensive part of an operation. For example, a truck that can move across unpaved roads costs approximately $50,000 U.S. dollars; its trailer may cost $15,000 to $20,000 or more. A 100-truck fleet with spare parts costs approximately $10 million, not including fuel, maintenance, or insurance.

Because it is so expensive, logistics is the most problematic aspect of a relief operation. It is the activity most subject to corruption, especially when the goods involved are in short supply. Whenever there are competing demands for food, fuel, and other relief supplies, then thefts, pilferage, and diversions can be expected.

Logistics operations may cost more than expected, because agencies are inexperienced in handling commodities or they are not familiar with the limitations of transportation or the complexities of the stages of a logistics system. In logistics, time equals money—when a procured commodity sits in a warehouse or on a ship, it costs the agency, although the commodity is not in motion. During the Ethiopian famine in 1985, the final cost of imported food doubled because of the long delays in the ports and attempts to transport it inland.

As vital as logistics activities are in an emergency-relief operation, there are few trained emergency logisticians. Most people handling logistics have gained their knowledge by trial and error, and many consistently make the same mistakes. A series of UN offices have attempted to provide coordination — UNDP Emergency Unit, the Department of Humanitarian Affairs, now the Office for Coordination of Humanitarian Assistance. These organizations have had varying rates of success in providing coordination, and sometimes are ignored by both UN line agencies and NGOs, who believe them superfluous or resent the attempt to insert leadership into a process which is already coordinated at the field level. Under the "lead UN agency" concept, one line agency (UNHCR, UNICEF, WFP) takes responsibility for providing coordination.

The Scope of Logistics

Logistics covers the movement of many items, but in famine operations, the movement of food is its primary and most important function. The movement of medical supplies, especially vaccines, is also important, but such shipments are usually much smaller and require specialized equipment and arrangements. Additional logistics activities include the movement of such items as tents, household supplies, fuel, and equipment. People are also moved from one site to another.

The Element of Time

A logistics operation has an important objective: the reduction of transit time, especially in the early stages of an emergency. Decisions are often made on the basis of time rather than cost, and time becomes the criterion against which all decisions are measured. In this sense, the time element is unique to emergency-relief logistics and makes it distinct from other forms of logistics operations.

Conceptualizing Logistics

Components of a Logistics System

Logistics is a set of interrelated components. The primary components are the physical elements of the system, or the *hardware*; the secondary components are the control system, sometimes called the *software.*

Primary components include warehouses and other storage places; transport such as trucks, planes, ships, and/or other carriers; and special structures such as fuel depots, garages, milling facilities, and cold-storage areas for perishables and medicines.

Secondary components include a *control system* consisting of:

- Procurement
- A monitoring system (waybills, call forwards, requisitions, et cetera) used to track the operation)
- People who coordinate the shipments and carry out checks and audits of the supplies in the system
- A distribution system that controls disbursement of commodities to the settlements

Model of a Typical Logistics System

Figure 11–1 (see next page) shows a conceptual model of a typical logistics system. The objective is to move supplies from their source (the suppliers, S) to their destination (the beneficiaries, B) (A).

Supplies are moved through a series of operations (called transport) (B) from one depot or warehouse to another (C).

When supplies are procured internationally, they are shipped from the supplier by truck or rail to a warehouse at the port of shipment, then transported by ship or in some cases by plane to another warehouse at the port of entry in the affected country. The commodities are cleared at the port of entry, transported to a regional warehouse, and then moved to a warehouse at a distribution point in the famine zone.

From the warehouse in the refugee camp, the commodities enter the distribution system and move directly to the beneficiaries (DS stands for distribution system) (D).

The overall system can be divided into three stages (D). The first stage goes from the supplier to the port of entry. The second stage is from the port, after the clearance of the cargo, to the final warehouses.

Figure 11-1

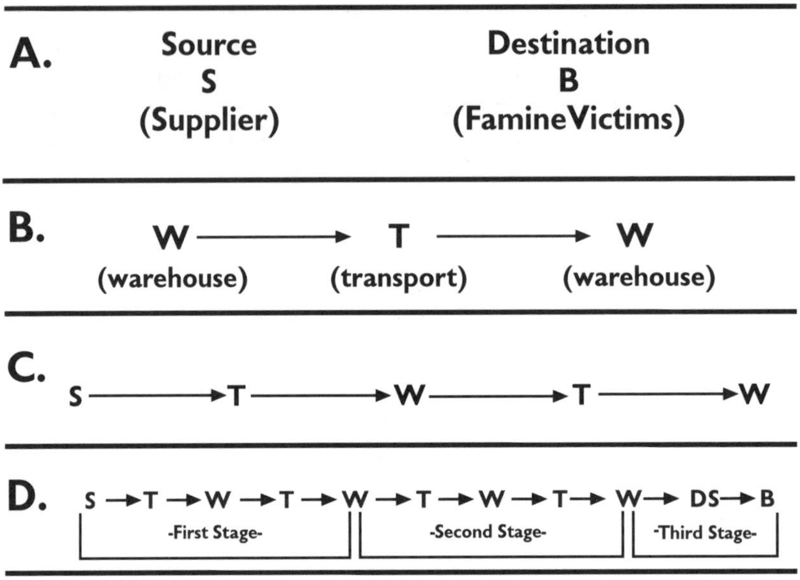

A. | Source | Destination
      | S | B
      | (Supplier) | (FamineVictims)

B. W ⟶ T ⟶ W
      (warehouse) (transport) (warehouse)

C. S ⟶ T ⟶ W ⟶ T ⟶ W

D. S → T → W → T → W → T → W → T → W → DS → B
      |—First Stage—| |—Second Stage—| |—Third Stage—|

In most cases, this is through an intermediate warehouse in the vicinity or region of the famine zone. The third stage goes from the camp warehouse through the distribution system to the beneficiaries.

Control Responsibilities

Responsibility for controlling logistics in the first stage lies with the procurement office. Control begins with the *specifications* of the order. The supplier is responsible for meeting the specifications, shipping the commodity, and delivering it in good shape to the port of entry. (Note: insurance does not usually extend beyond the port of entry. For this reason, the supplier usually will not accept responsibility for the cargo after a relief agency or its agents have accepted it at the port of entry.)

Once the shipment has been cleared, the consignee, usually a relief agency, takes responsibility for shipping it onward; thus, the *humanitarian agency* is responsible for control in the second stage. Most of the effort and problems occur during the second stage, primarily because agencies are not adequately prepared for this task. Ideally, responsibility for control is vested in a person known as the *traffic director*. The traffic director controls delivery schedules, assignment of supplies, and decisions regarding when to ship from the port of entry to intermediate warehouses. The traffic director is usually the chief logistician and, in some situations, may be the local procurement officer.

In the third stage—distribution to people—local government officials or the relief-agency field staff are responsible for control.

Local Procurement

The above descriptions cover a full-scale international logistics system. There is, however, a way to significantly reduce and simplify logistics: local procurement. Local procurement eliminates all of the first stage and most of the second. It is often possible to contract with local suppliers to deliver needed commodities directly to the distribution points.

Logistics Coordination

The most important person in a logistics operation is the traffic director, whose responsibilities include:

- Controlling procurement and distribution
- Controlling transport, the allocation of trucks or other vehicles, and their destinations
- Monitoring warehouses
- Directing allocations of supplies to intermediate warehouses and from there to camps
- Planning the overall distribution system in cooperation with camp administrators

The traffic director must be based in the field, have sufficient cars or aircraft to move up and down the system from the distribution points to the port of entry, and be able to control the fuel allocation for the vehicles. Ideally, the traffic director is an experienced logistician from an agency that has extensive experience in moving large quantities of supplies. In addition, he should be completely familiar with priorities in a relief operation. In summary, the traffic director should be the focal point for all coordination in a logistics system.

Decision Making

The need to make early logistics decisions in an emergency cannot be overemphasized. Early decisions save money and lives. This is especially true for food and medical supplies. The longer basic decisions are delayed, the greater the cost. For instance, if it takes two months from the time food is ordered until it is delivered to the distribution point, delaying a decision to procure and ship food by even a week means that a portion of the food may have to be sent by air, increasing the cost perhaps tenfold. If the decision is delayed longer, it may not be possible to meet all the needs. As a result, people may die, unless alternate sources of food can be found.

System Planning

At the beginning of an emergency, planners should conceptualize and plan the entire logistics system. It is important to define the key roles and responsibilities of all personnel at each stage and to put together the records and controls to monitor the flow of supplies through the system. Too often, organizations attempt to set up the system in a piecemeal fashion, resulting in confusion, delays, and higher costs.

Logistics Controls

Various types of documents are used to control commodities in the logistics system. As supplies go down the system from supplier to destination, the documents include:

- *Waybills* (bills of lading). These shipping documents are used to control the shipment during transport.
- *Stock control cards* and *warehouse records*. These documents control the supplies while they are in a warehouse.
- *Ration cards*. These provide the primary commodity control within the distribution system.

The paperwork that controls the flow or rate of movement of supplies while they are in the system consists of:

- *Call forwards*. These documents are issued to summon supplies already in the system.
- *Requisitions*. These documents call for supplies that need to be ordered or sent from a buffer stock further up the system.
- *Purchase orders* or *contracts*. Procurement officers issue them to suppliers to initiate the purchase of supplies not already in the system.

The Primary Documents

The two documents that control first-stage and second-stage logistics are the waybill and the stock card.

Waybills are used to record the cargoes being shipped, to certify they have been received by the transporter in good shape, and to indicate they are being delivered in the same shape and quantity as received.

Normally, a waybill will have an original plus three or four copies. When a transporter delivers the supplies to a warehouse, the waybill is signed and the transporter uses a copy as his invoice for payment. The shipper at the point of origin and the warehouseman at the destination keep other copies. Additional copies are used to notify the traffic director that the goods have arrived at the specified location.

Stock cards are the primary way of controlling supplies in the warehouse. They provide a storage account and a record of when supplies are delivered and the frequency of delivery and withdrawal of each type of good. One card is usually kept for each type of item in the warehouse.

Accountability

All parties should clearly understand the chain of accountability in a logistics system. In the warehouse, the accountable person is the *store-keeper*. During transport, accountability lies with the *driver* or person conveying the commodity.

Responsibility during shipment is transferred from the storekeeper to the driver by means of a waybill and from the driver to the next storekeeper with a receipted waybill.

Checkers should be used at each transfer point to check the goods loaded or discharged and certify all are accounted for. Damages or losses should be recorded on the receipted waybill, indicating overage, short-age, or damage. Again, the driver is responsible for shortages or damages in transit.

Role of Procurement in Logistics Control

The role of procurement in logistics control is often not clearly un-derstood, even by procurement officers. Control begins when technical specifications are established for the items to be purchased. These speci-fications establish the quality of the commodity.

Other decisions made at the time of procurement also affect quality and the likely condition of the supplies when they arrive at their desti-nation. For example, specifications regarding packaging of foods can determine how well they travel, the percentage of loss that can be ex-pected en route, and how long the commodity can be maintained in a destination warehouse. What may appear to be a minor decision about the type of bag to use for food—cloth or polypropylene—can have a major effect on shelf life and transportation requirements.

In most international relief organizations, procurement offices are located in the organization's headquarters. In fact, procurement offic-ers are often far removed and sometimes unacquainted with conditions in the field. Unless the field staff provides clear, thorough specifica-tions, complications are likely to develop. Therefore, it is extremely important for the procurement process to begin with requests from the field. Ideally, procurement officers or personnel thoroughly briefed in procurement procedures should be assigned to the logistics team in the field, and they should be given the responsibility for preparing the pro-curement specifications. The primary role of a procurement officer at headquarters would then be to facilitate requests from the field. This is undoubtedly difficult, given donor pressures and the reality of donor constraints, but it is important for organizations to strive to focus their procurement activities at the field level.

Storage Facilities and Equipment

Warehousing

Selection of warehousing is important, since relief supplies are likely to spend a significant amount of time in these facilities.

- *Size.* The warehouse must be large enough to store the types and quantities of supplies being stockpiled. If a variety of goods is being stored in one place, the warehouse plan should be based on the most bulky commodity.

  Food grains usually require more space than other relief commodities. As a rule of thumb, one ton of grain usually occupies a floor space of one square meter and a volumetric space of one cubic meter. Calculating the amount of storage space needed is easy: if 500 tons of grain is to be stored, for example, a warehouse of approximately 500 cubic meters of storage space is required.

- *Permanent Buildings.* When storing grain, it is usually best to select permanent buildings with hard-surfaced (preferably concrete) floors. Almost any type of building can be used for storage, but those with minimal windows and large access doors are usually best—fewer windows reduce the likelihood of theft. Grains should not be stored on the second floor, since few structures have been designed to withstand heavy weight.

  In remote locations, relief camps, or feeding centers, it may be necessary to construct temporary warehouses. In some situations, adequate supplies of local materials may be available for building warehouses. Wherever time and weather conditions permit, small-scale warehouses can be built using local resources and employing the beneficiaries and/or local labor.

- *Prefab Structures.* The use of prefabricated, flexible, plastic warehouses is increasing in emergencies, and many models are now available. The warehouse should be selected on the basis of its demonstrated wind resistance and climatic suitability. Before procuring a prefabricated warehouse, the method of anchoring it to the ground should be determined. In 1985, one-third of the warehouses procured for emergency-relief operations in eastern Sudan were destroyed within a two-week period, because they were insufficiently anchored and were unable to withstand high winds.

- *Selection Criteria.* Other than space, the main consideration for warehouses is the amount of protection they provide for the items stored. Within the storage enclosure, commodities must be protected from:
  - The climatic environment
  - Theft
  - Rodents and other pests

- *Organization.* Warehouses should be well organized. Different commodities must be clearly identifiable, and all supplies must be within easy reach. Warehouses should be organized on a first-in, first-out basis, so that food and medicines can be kept as fresh as possible.

- *Controls.* Access to warehouses must be managed. Ideally, controls begin outside the building with a fence, good lighting, and a monitored gate. Within the warehouse, controls include regulating visitor access to the building and having interior lighting and limited access to the supplies by people entering the building. At a minimum, workers who are authorized to enter should have some identification.

  Stock controls, stock cards, and other key paperwork should be available from the beginning, and warehouse operators should be thoroughly familiar with the proper use of the control documents.

Storage Equipment

Plastic sheeting and canvas tarpaulins are the most common way to provide additional protection for goods in storage. Both give only moderate protection against moisture and none against insects or rodents.

Two items are available to help store food grains in temperate or dry climates: *bulk-grain silos* and *storage cubes*. These containers are ideal for relief operations. They are light and easy to transport and move once they are on site. The containers are gas tight and made of a plastic sheet 0.83 mm in thickness, and they can withstand solar ultraviolet irradiation for long periods. The storage containers are hermetically sealed, which gives them a major advantage over conventional plastic silos or other grain-storage systems. When the hermetic containers are sealed, the oxygen concentration drops to between 6 percent and 8 percent, and carbon dioxide concentrations rise to approximately 11 percent. Insects and fungi cannot survive in the bag, and costly and potentially hazardous fumigation is unnecessary.

Rodents can gnaw through most synthetic materials, including polyvinyl chloride, or PVC, a plastic used for liners. However, the design of the containers and the way the material lies over the grain provide slippery surfaces that make it difficult for rodents to chew.

Two basic designs are available: a circular silo to store unbagged grains in bulk and a cubical container to store bagged grains. The silos are made in sizes from fifty metric tons to 1,000 metric tons, while the storage cubes are usually produced in sizes corresponding to truck-bed cargo loads (ten to fifty tons).

The designs enable the containers to be used in various ways. Some common uses of the silos include:

- *Auxiliary Dockside Storage.* Large 500-ton to 1,000-ton silos can be used to provide temporary bulk storage at ports when inland transport cannot clear food from the wharves promptly. With these units, costly port congestion can be relieved and spoilage of food on the wharves can be prevented.

- *Overflow Storage at Regional Logistics Bases.* Silos can be used to provide additional storage for unbagged grains at regional food-storage depots or distribution centers. To relieve port congestion and bagging delays, bulk grains can be moved inland on lorries, transferred to storage silos, and then bagged at a regional depot or distribution center.

- *Storage of Locally Procured Grains.* Silos can also be used to store or protect grain in camps or settlements where supplies are procured locally or where famine victims produce a portion of their food needs. (They were originally designed to improve village grain storage and to reduce losses.) Since the silos are hermetically sealed, destruction from moisture, insects, and rodents is minimized.

Storage cubes may be used for:

- *Temporary Dockside Storage of Bagged Grains.* Cubes can provide temporary, safe, weatherproof storage space for bagged grains at overcrowded wharves until food can be transported inland. They can be obtained in sizes corresponding to the loads carried by lorries to facilitate logistical scheduling and loading.

- *Temporary Storage at Forward Warehouses or at Distribution Centers.* The cubes can provide additional safe storage for bagged grains until they can be distributed or placed in conventional warehouses.

- *Point Storage for Cross-line or Cross-border Logistics.* Cubes can be used at staging areas when food is sent into conflict zones, where conventional storage facilities are not practical. Food can be off-loaded directly into the cubes, which remain sealed until needed.

Cold-storage and Cold-chain Facilities

A cold chain must be established, if vaccines are needed for an immunization program. Cold-chain logistics is a special branch of emergency logistics, one that is almost always problematic. Some vaccines must be maintained within a specific temperature range from the time they are produced until the time they are injected into patients. Anytime the temperature goes above or below that range, the vaccines can be damaged and lose their effectiveness. To establish a cold chain, certain types of equipment and facilities are required, including:

- *Cold-storage rooms* at national or regional warehouses
- *Sealed cold boxes* for transporting the vaccines
- *Self-powered refrigerators* or vaccine bins to store vaccines in the camps

The most common break in a cold chain occurs when vaccines are shipped or stored in containers that are also used for food and beverages for relief workers. As people open and close the containers to get something to eat or drink, temperatures inside fluctuate from the critical levels, and the vaccines are damaged. All vaccine-storage facilities should be used only for that purpose. WHO will provide a current list of companies that supply cold-chain equipment and approved cold boxes for emergencies. These can be obtained from:

> World Health Organization
> 20 Avenue Appia
> 1211 Geneva 27, Switzerland
>
> or
>
> Emergency Preparedness and Disaster Coordination Unit
> Pan American Health Organization
> 525 Twenty-third Street NW
> Washington, DC 20037 USA

Forward Logistics Bases

In an emergency operation, it is often necessary to set up new logistics bases to simplify supply operations in or adjacent to the famine zone (the forward areas). These bases can usually be established quickly, especially if existing buildings are available to use as warehouses. If suitable buildings cannot be found, storage cubes may be used until prefab warehouses are erected.

The minimal requirements for a forward base are:

- Adequate warehouses
- Storage cubes or tarpaulins to protect stockpiles
- Fuel depot
- Vehicle workshop
- Radio, telephone, or telex communications

The site for the base is determined by the type or types of transport needed to deliver supplies to and from the base. A railhead or major road junction is usually a good location. The most important factor, however, is the amount of time required to deliver goods in the forward area. In other words, the decision should be made not only on distance (the site physically closest to the areas to be served), but also on the amount of time it takes to travel that distance (the site with the best access to those areas).

A checklist of equipment and facilities for a forward logistics base is found in Table 11–A at the end of this chapter.

Figure 11–2

Temporary Storage for Distribution Centers or Refugee Camps

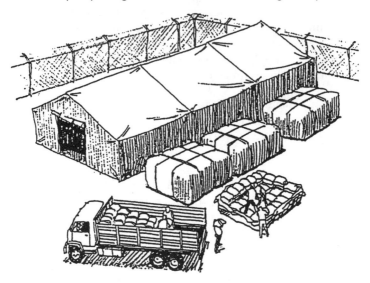

Point Storage for Cross-line Food Logistics

Transport

As mentioned earlier, transportation is the most expensive part of a relief operation. Thus, it is important to select the most appropriate form of transport for specific commodities.

Cargo Factors

The first consideration is weight, which is the primary limiting factor in all forms of transport. The heavier a commodity, the more expensive it is to transport and the more rugged and slower the form of transport.

The second consideration is volume. Items that are light in weight but large in volume eat up expensive transportation resources quickly. For example, plastic jerry cans are often in demand in a relief operation. They are lightweight—a thousand weigh only one ton—but thirty cans take up a lot of space—one cubic meter.

Most logistics planners use *cubing out* to determine the most appropriate type of *transport*—they try to strike the right balance between the volume and the weight of an item. This is extremely important when choosing cargoes to transport by air.

Transport Efficiencies

Ships/barges are the most cost-efficient transport, but they are usually the slowest. Aircraft are the most costly. Shipping by rail over long distances is usually more cost efficient than in lorries. The longer the distance, the more efficient. However, lorries are still needed at both ends of the rail line.

While railways are more cost efficient than lorries and can sometimes reach areas in the rainy season that trucks cannot, railways are more problematic in the third world. In an emergency, when timeliness is crucial, it may be more advantageous to ship by lorry than by rail. If one truck breaks down, there are still others likely to get through, but if one locomotive breaks down, twenty railway carriages can be stopped indefinitely.

In remote areas, particularly mountainous ones, pack animals may be more practical than trucks or other forms of transport. Mules imported from the United States, for example, provided a significant amount of transportation for food assistance in Afghanistan.

Criteria for Selecting Vehicles

Important considerations when selecting vehicles include:

- Distance to be traveled
- Terrain
- Road conditions
- Whether streams must be forded
- Load-carrying capacity of bridges en route
- Fuel efficiency
- Compatibility of the vehicle with maintenance in the country and the availability of parts

Determining Fleet Size

In determining the number of vehicles to be used for a mission, it is important to consider:

- Time en route and turnaround
- Load-carrying capacity of the vehicles
- Total tonnage needed to serve the target population

Logistics Staff

Successful implementation depends on a good logistics staff, but most operations are understaffed. A good system requires many people, including a traffic director, procurement coordinator, transport coordinator, fuel coordinator, forward logistics officer, inventory-control officers, accountants, warehouse staff, procurement officer, and maintenance officers. Control will be lost (and so will commodities) if too few qualified people are used.

Equipment

Critical equipment in a relief-logistics operation includes telecommunications, control forms, forklifts (special forklifts may be necessary to unload planes), pallets, and spare parts for vehicles.

Air Transport

Large military-cargo aircraft and wide-body jumbo jets have made it commonplace for relief organizations to ship cargoes by air in the early stages of an emergency. But this often makes little sense, since many of these shipments consist of items available locally or for which local substitutes could be found. With basic health programs, such as UNICEF's Expanded Program of Immunization, even the need for sending vaccines has greatly diminished, since adequate stockpiles have been developed in most countries.

Air transport is both costly and, ultimately, of little sustainable impact. Even the largest jet transports such as the Boeing 747 and Lockheed C-5 Galaxy have negligible cargo-carrying capacity when compared to other forms of transport. The C-130 Hercules and the Antonov An-28, the most popular transports used in relief operations, can carry only a maximum of about twenty tons of food, an amount equivalent to the capacity of one medium-sized lorry without a trailer. The C-130 will burn approximately ten tons of fuel during a typical flight of 1,000 kilometers. At an average cost of $1,000 per ton, fuel alone will cost about $10,000 to deliver supplies. Compare this to a shipping cost of $55 per ton by sea or $25 per ton by lorry. Clearly, air shipments make little sense, unless the cargo is needed immediately to save lives.

Figure 11–3

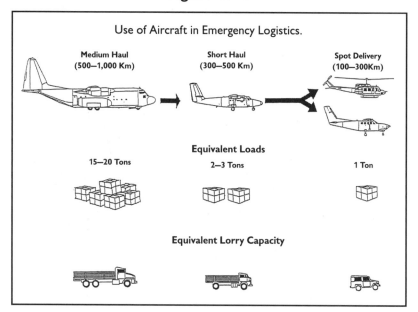

Use of Aircraft in Emergency Logistics.

Despite the costs, there are often tremendous pressures on relief agencies to fly in supplies during an emergency. Donor governments often make military transport available to humanitarian organizations at little or no cost. In these circumstances, the following principles may be followed in using aircraft:

- In first-stage logistics:
  - Use the largest plane available. Ideal civilian aircraft are the Boeing 747, DC-10, L-1011, DC-8F, or Boeing 707. Military aircraft include the C-5 and C-141 transports. Avoid the smaller tactical transports like the C-130 or C-160 Transall for long international flights.
  - Land as close as possible to the famine zone.
  - Ship only items of verified high priority such as measles vaccines or equipment that will facilitate operations such as radios, light vehicles, and prefabricated warehouses.
  - If foods must be shipped, choose those that will provide the highest calories and energy per unit of weight. Avoid sending basic grains. Instead, send blended-grain foods, because they will maximize the protein, helping the body.
- In second-stage logistics, use aircraft only when all other means have failed. If planes must be used, the following principles may apply:

- Generally, the shorter the distance, the more practical the airlift (the aircraft will need to carry less fuel and therefore can carry more cargo).
- Avoid using helicopters. They are costly to operate and have a low carrying capacity. Helicopters should only be used to ship supplies over short areas and into remote or isolated sites.
- The C-130, the French-German C-160 Transall, and smaller aircraft are more practical in second-stage logistics, since the flights are over shorter distances, less fuel is required, and more cargo can be carried. Planes like the C-130 were originally designed as tactical transports to land on relatively short, unimproved strips.

In summary, if someone else is paying for the aircraft, use them. But remember, it will still be necessary to use trucks at both ends of the flight.

Operational Lessons and Suggestions

Problems to Expect

Certain problems tend to occur frequently in a logistics operation. The most common are:

1. *Problems in Stage 1*:
   - Procurement delays. These delays usually result from bidding procedures, confusion about specifications, or lack of clarity in field requests.
   - Donor pressures to accept substitutes
   - Acquisition of materials that were not requested and are unsuitable for the local situation, climate, or terrain
2. *Problems in Stage 2*:
   - Customs delays such as paperwork and clearances
   - Congestion at the port on arrival
   - Inland transport delays
   - Theft and pilferage
   - Losses due to improper storage or inadequate protection of commodities while in storage. Rations for 250,000 people were destroyed by one rainstorm in Ethiopia in 1985.
   - Materials-handling delays (off-loading bulk grains and bagging operations at the port)
   - Losses from lack of insurance coverage
3. *Problems in Stage 3*:
   - Inadequate storage facilities at the destination
   - Inadequate means of protecting supplies while in storage
   - Lack of suitable milling equipment

- Theft and pilferage
- Problems with registration/disbursement procedures

Selecting a Logistics Agency

It is often difficult to designate a lead agency for managing a multiagency logistics operation. There are several options:

- Hiring a private firm
- Designating an NGO
- Selecting an experienced UN agency such as UNICEF. (WFP, a UN agency that provides food to third-world countries or to regions in conflict, usually delivers only to the port or regional center. Governments or NGOs are responsible for inland transfer.)

Operational Hints

The following operation hints may help:

1. Always have adequate *buffer stocks* of supplies on hand to cover times when logistics operations are unable to keep up with demand and unanticipated emergencies. Plan for an oversupply of 20 percent to 50 percent in an emergency.

2. Buy locally. Local purchase is an important and underused resource. Wherever available, locally purchased supplies can provide significant advantages including:
    - Saving time
    - Saving money
    - Bridging gaps until other supplies arrive
    - Providing a buffer against supply irregularities
    - Stimulating the local economy

3. Simplify the system. The objective is to reduce the number of stops and transfers. This speeds up the operation and reduces theft. Even if simplification increases operational costs, it will eventually reduce the amount of money spent.

4. Consolidate facilities to avoid unnecessary loading and unloading or extra staffing.

5. Unify the logistics system. For example, where there are several organizations simultaneously ordering and distributing food in a large operation, unify purchasing and shipping procedures.

6. Create redundancy in transport. If the operation depends on railroads, for example, the loss of one bridge can halt an entire operation. It is necessary to have a backup system to deliver supplies.

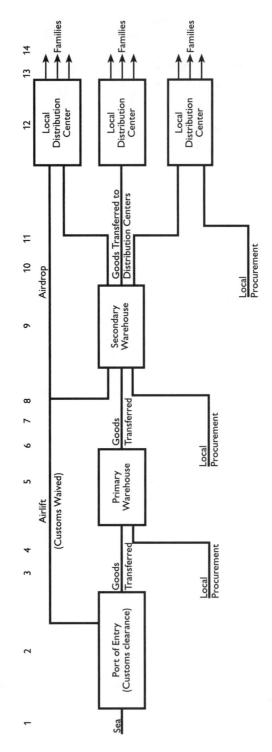

Figure 11-4

SCHEMATIC OF LOGISTIC SYSTEM AND EXPECTED DELAYS

Figure 11-4 (continued)

1.–Procurement delays
 –Shipping delays

2.–Clearance delays
 –Pilferage
 –Diversions by local gov.
 –Spoilage

3.–Transport delays
 –Enroute pilferage
4.–Procurement delays
 –Poor quality goods

5.–Pilferage
 –Spoilage
 –Lost in bureaucracy
 –Forgotten

6.–Bureaucratic losses
7.–Enroute pilferage
 –Thefts
 –Spoilage
8.–Procurement delays
 –Poor quality goods
 –Transport delays

9.–Pilferage
 –Spoilage
 –Lost in the records
 –Forgotten
 –Mismarked

10.–Enroute pilferage
 –Thefts
11.–Unavailability of goods
 –Insufficient quantities
 –Poor quality of goods

12.–Pilferage
 –Thefts

13.–Inequitable distribution
 –Hoarding
 –Diversion by village leaders

14.–Unsuitability to people's needs
 –Culturally unsuitable
 –Over-rapid consumption
 –Insufficient quantities to meet needs

Notes:

A way to speed delivery at the port of entry is to establish the warehouse at or adjacent to the customs shed at the wharf or airport and off-load directly from the carrier to the warehouse.

One way to speed deliveries through the system and reduce losses may be to eliminate the Secondary Warehouse and ship goods directly to the villages.

One way to reduce food losses, increase consumption, and make stocks easier to monitor is to provide limited rations. For example, a ten-day ration is smaller; thus easier to monitor, and people will not be as likely to hoard that amount. Over consumption by malnourished people will not be as critical (i.e., if they eat all their food in the first seven days, they will only be out of food for three days until the next distribution).

7. Define the area of operation. Headquarters of most agencies are likely to be in the capital, but operations are usually in a remote area. Traffic directors should be located in the area of operation, where key commodities are needed or being moved. The area of operation usually extends from the port of entry to the distribution points and includes all communications and transport facilities inside that area.

8. Standardize equipment, especially trucks. This is difficult when donors want to provide trucks from their own countries, but it is extremely important to standardize vehicles, particularly for repair.

9. Make small, manageable shipments to the distribution points. Shipments should be a size that can be controlled and not consumed by people too rapidly.

10. Standardize and minimize supplies. A key concept in logistics management is standardizing the types of supplies and equipment being used and keeping the number of articles in a system to a minimum. The first thing a logistics consultant will usually do is reduce the number of supplies in the system until logistics management controls are in place and working well.

Controlling Transport Costs

One of the major problems is keeping the cost of transport at acceptable levels. Often, local contractors raise prices to intolerable levels when they know an emergency exists and a relief organization has few other options for delivering commodities.

To control transport prices, the relief agency has three options:

- Purchasing a fleet of vehicles and setting up an independent transport operation. This is usually a costly option and requires the agency to manage and maintain the trucking fleet.

- Purchasing trucks and then reselling them to local operators on a work-equity basis. This approach, known as *captive contracting*, still requires an investment in the vehicles but places the burden of maintenance on the purchaser/operator. These programs are usually popular, and the trucks can be amortized over a period of several years. In return for work-equity agreements, the purchaser agrees to provide transport services at fixed prices for a specified period. An added benefit of captive contracting: the vehicles are usually maintained better than when they are operated by the relief agency. The prospective owners have a vested interest in maintaining the vehicles.

- Purchasing used trucks that have been reconditioned

Rules of Thumb for Logistics Operations

The following suggestions may improve a logistics operation:

- Use trucks for distances less than 500 kilometers and rail for longer distances
- Do not build roads for food supplies. Instead, build up buffer stocks. The only time to build roads for a transport system is when water tankers are being operated. Improving patches in the road, however, could speed supplies.
- Mill grains at the point of use (camps or settlements). This will eliminate the need for a complex unloading, bagging, and reloading operation further up the logistics chain and in some cases can prolong the life of the grain.
- The need for transporting supplies by air occurs in the early stages of an operation, not later on
- If a portion of the food supplies must be purchased overseas, buy the general ration abroad and supplemental food from internal sources, if fresh foods of good quality are available.
- In Africa, it may be necessary to import foods for a large-scale operation, especially those related to conflicts. In the rest of the world, food can usually be purchased locally.

Table 11-A
Equipment and Facilities for Forward Logistics Bases

1. Site Preparation
   Grading and leveling
   Road improvements
     Surfacing
     Culverts
     Drainage

2. Office Buildings
   Permanent
   Prefab, metal
   Tent

3. Office Equipment
   Desks
   Chairs
   Photocopier
   File cabinet
   Bookshelves
   Expendable equipment
   Office supplies

4. Warehousing
   Permanent
   Prefab, metal 1,000 metric tons (mt)
   Prefab, metal 500 mt
   Prefab, plastic 1,000 mt
   Prefab, plastic 500 mt

5. Storage Equipment
   Silos 1,000 mt
   Silos 250 mt
   Silos 100 mt
   Storage cubes 100 mt
   Storage cubes 50 mt
   Storage cubes 20 mt
   Storage cubes 5 mt
   Carts/trolleys
   Forklift
   Storage shelves
   Plastic sheeting
   Other_____

6. Radio Room

Permanent
Prefab, metal
Tent

7. Communications Equipment
   Radio
   Telephone
   Intercom
   Telex
   Fax
   Walkie-talkies

8. Workshop
   Permanent
   Prefab, metal
   Prefab, plastic

9. Working Equipment
   _____
   _____

10. Other Work Buildings
    Permanent
    Prefab, metal
    Prefab, plastic

11. Other Work Equipment
    _____
    _____

12. Fuel Depot
    Storage tank(s)
    Pumps, hoses, fittings
    Defueling stand
    Barrel-storage area
    Fire-fighting equipment

13. Airfield/Heliopad
    Furnishings
    Strip grading/leveling
    Fueling station
      Bladders
      Storage tank
      Pump (hand)
      Pump (motorized)
    Radio beacon
    Landing lights
    VHF radio

14. Security Facilities
    Guardhouses

Fencing
Gates

15. Electrical System
    Generator
    Wiring
    Poles
    Light standards
    Fuel for generator

16. Water System
    Deep well (borehole)
    Submersible pump
    Storage tank
    Shallow well
    Hand pump
    Pipes
    Outlets
    Taps

17. Sanitation System
    Toilets
    Showers
    Incinerator

18. Housing
    Permanent
    Prefab
    Tent

19. Residential
    Beds
    Tables
    Chairs
    Personal storage
    Other

20. Mess Hall/Kitchen
    Refrigerator
    Stove
    Wash racks
    Gas
    Utensils
    Pots and pans
    Tables
    Chairs
    Other _____

21. Miscellaneous Facilities
    _____
    _____

12 | *Assessment and Monitoring*

Introduction

From the beginning of a relief operation to its conclusion, a variety of information needs to be collected to guide program planning and execution. These processes are called *assessment* and *monitoring*. Assessment is used to determine the situation and the possible responses. Monitoring is the ongoing evaluation of the interventions. A clear understanding of the interventions that are available and the most appropriate time to use them should guide the collection of information. If an agency is planning to use conventional food-aid approaches, food availability and food logistics are important issues. If the agency chooses an income-support approach, the assessment must identify potential projects and determine the financial mechanisms that can be used. Most importantly, the assessment must decide whether the income-support approach can get adequate food supplies into problem areas in the time available.

The assessment and monitoring process usually has three stages. It begins with a reconnaissance of the area to determine the overall situation. This provides information to guide the first relief response. But more importantly, this reconnaissance is the first step in a continual monitoring process. It is necessarily a brief overview, based mainly on observations by the assessment team, and relies on trained or experienced observers who look for indicators of problems.

After the initial reconnaissance is completed and programs are being established, relief agencies collect more detailed data about the situation. In this, they may collect statistics from their programs or carry out sample surveys to compile more detailed information. This provides program staff with information for adjusting their programs.

Importance of Assessment

Rapid, accurate assessment is the key to a successful initial response. The purposes of an assessment are:

- To determine people's needs
- To help set priorities for action
- To provide data for program planning

The importance of an accurate assessment cannot be overstated. A swift, accurate, credible assessment will enable relief managers to proceed quickly and efficiently. An incomplete or inaccurate assessment—one that does not address major needs or provide misleading data—may lead to inappropriate responses and costly delays.

Variations of Data Requirements

Assessments and assessment-information needs vary according to the group doing them. Host governments, international food agencies such as the WFP, donor governments, and NGOs may carry out these evaluations. Those done by governments and international organizations tend to be more comprehensive, because their interests are wider. NGO surveys tend to be more problem focused, on such issues as health and nutrition.

Types of Assessments

There are usually five types of assessments.

1. A *situation assessment* (also known as initial reconnaissance) is the immediate estimate of the overall situation. It determines the extent of the famine, locates the area of critical need, and identifies health threats. In the initial stages of a famine, relief agencies must respond according to certain assumptions. Therefore, one of the most important functions of this initial reconnaissance is verifying that assumptions are correct and, if not, developing the data needed to adjust the initial response.

2. A *needs assessment* is a determination of the needs of people. These are usually classified as immediate needs, which concern health, life support, and protection, and long-term needs, which are economic and agricultural requirements.

3. Sector or *activity assessments* are evaluations of the needs in specific sectors (such as food, health, and nutrition). One of the most important activity assessments deals with logistics.

4. A *resource assessment* determines what is available within the country to support the relief operations and the impact that large-scale use of these resources might have on the local economy. This helps planners determine the aid levels required.

5. *Epidemiological surveillance* is the early identification of threats to public health precipitated or aggravated by the famine and the establishment of a monitoring and medical response to identify, isolate, and eliminate any health problems.

Elements of Assessment

An assessment can be divided into six activities:

1. *Preparedness Planning.* An accurate assessment depends on thorough planning and preparation. The information needed can be identified well in advance. The methods for collecting the necessary data and the selection of formats for collection and presentation of the information should be established as part of the organization's general emergency-preparedness activities. By preparing to undertake assessments well in advance of an emergency, all potential information needs can be identified and adequate procedures and methodologies can be developed. Standard survey techniques, questionnaires, checklists, and procedures should be prepared to ensure all areas are examined and the information is reported using standard terminology and classification.

2. *Survey and Data Collection.* The gathering of the information must proceed rapidly and thoroughly. In an initial reconnaissance, surveyors should look for patterns and indicators of potential problems. Using the procedures developed earlier, key problem areas are thoroughly checked.

3. *Interpretation.* Thorough analysis of the information gathered is critical. Those doing the analysis must be trained to detect and recognize indicators of problems, to interpret the information, and to link the information to action programs.

4. *Forecasting.* Using the collected data, the assessment team must develop estimates on how the situation might develop, so contingency plans can be drawn. Forecasting can benefit from many specialists, especially those who have had extensive experience in emergencies and who might be able to detect trends and provide insights as to what course an emergency might follow.

5. *Reporting.* When data analysis and forecasts are complete, the results need to be disseminated. Reports should be prepared in a format that enables managers to prepare plans and projects. Essential information should be presented and structured, so the main patterns and trends are clear.

6. *Monitoring.* An assessment is not an end result. It is one part of a continuing process. The initial assessment should provide baseline data and a basis for further monitoring. Data systems must be set up, so relief officials can determine whether a situation is improving or deteriorating. The systems should also provide a way to measure the effectiveness of relief activities. Each assessment or survey should be designed so it builds upon previous surveys and expands the database.

Assessment Methods

Several methods can be used to carry out assessments. The two most common are:

1. *On-site Visual Inspections by Trained Observers.* Qualified, experienced observers can often interview key personnel on site and visually review the people, their condition, and the sites where they are situated. From their inspection, the observers can prepare estimates about the scope and magnitude of the situation. Visual examinations, however, have their drawbacks. Some major problems cannot be detected by simple observation. What one cannot see is often more important than what is visible. For example, death rates, which are the most important indicator of stress in a population, cannot be determined from observation. In many societies, childhood diseases and malnutrition cannot be detected without detailed surveys, since families routinely keep those children out of the sight of strangers. In one classic case in East Africa, a survey team reported all was fine in a settlement, because it saw no malnourished children. A simple survey would have shown all the children had died.

2. *Surveys.* Simple surveys based on interviews with villagers in the affected areas and statistical information from registration forms at health and feeding centers can provide information that can be used to plan projects. Usually, sample surveys can indicate people's immediate needs and health and nutritional status.

   A key assessment activity that must be carried out by survey is the first health and nutrition assessment. This survey provides the information needed to establish the baseline data, that is, points of reference, for disease surveillance and for evaluation of nutritional progress.

Approaches to Assessment

Assessments may be broad in scope or focus on certain aspects. *Comprehensive assessments* collect information about every aspect of an emergency. Relief authorities must weigh the importance of each set of problems in deciding where to assign priorities. Comprehensive assessments are usually carried out by the agencies that have overall emergency responsibilities, such as the government of the country. These exercises require extensive information gathering and usually take longer to complete than sector assessments. But if they are properly planned and executed, they provide invaluable information. A comprehensive assessment establishes priorities, its primary result.

Critical sector assessments focus on those sectors needed to save lives: food, water, public health and immunizations, and sanitation.

The Keys to Successful Assessment

To design a successful and accurate assessment, planners should:

1. *Identify the users.* Every element of an assessment can be designed to collect information for a specific user. The potential users can specify their data needs during the design phase. For example, health workers need some types of information that will only be useful in certain formats, usually tables, while a procurement officer will need quantitative or statistical data.

2. *Identify information needed to plan specific programs.* Assessments too often collect information that is incomplete or is of little value for planning relief programs or specific interventions. In many cases, information is anecdotal rather than substantive. In others, valuable time is wasted collecting detailed information when representative data would be as useful. Determine what information is key, the method that needs to be used to develop the data, and how much and how detailed it needs to be. The type of assistance an agency usually provides should be considered when listing the data to be collected. For example, an agency that provides food will need to know about availability of transport, fuel, and road conditions, among other things.

3. *Determine the best places to obtain accurate information.* If the information must be obtained from sample surveys, it is important the areas to be surveyed provide an accurate picture of needs and priorities. For example, carrying out a health survey in a medical center would yield a distorted view of the overall health situation, since only sick or severely malnourished people would be canvassed.

4. *Consider the format.* It is important to present the data in a form useful to analysts and program planners—one that makes the implications clear, so priorities can be set quickly. Laptop computers with integrated spreadsheets and graphics make it possible to present pertinent information in graphic form. By applying baselines and standards to the presentation, key relationships can be quickly noted. For example, daily death rates should be calculated and compared to the international standard of 1.0 deaths per 10,000 people per day.

5. *Consider the timing of the assessment.* Timing can affect the accuracy of the assessment, since situations and needs can change dramatically day to day, and information needs to be collected when it is available and most useful. Relief needs are always relative, but as a general rule, initial surveys should be broad in scope and determine overall patterns and trends. More detailed information can wait until emergency operations are well established.

6. *Distinguish emergency from chronic needs.* Virtually all developing countries have long-standing, chronic needs in most sectors. The assessment should be designed so analysts can distinguish between chronic and emergency needs. For example, malnutrition may be prevalent in the country in normal times. Therefore, a nutrition survey will almost certainly reflect poor nutritional status. The surveyors must differentiate between what is normal for the location and what is not, so that emergency assistance and health care can be provided to those most in need. Assessments may bring to light previously unrecognized or unacknowledged problems in a society. Thus, the data-collection system can carefully structure the information, so critical information such as health status can be used for long-term planning.

7. *Use recognized standards, terminology, and procedures.* Assessments will invariably be carried out by a variety of people operating independently. To provide a basis for evaluating the information, the assessment must be reported using standard terminology, ratings, and classifications. Standard survey forms that give clear guidelines for descriptive terms are usually the best way to ensure all information is reported on a uniform basis.

It will be difficult to differentiate between chronic and emergency needs without having baseline data accepted and recognized and realistic standards in each sector.

Baseline data are normally used as a reference in health and nutrition programs. For example, health officials must know the prevalence of the disease in the community in normal times to determine whether there is an increase in the number or severity of cases.

Reference data are usually used instead of baseline data to establish a point of reference from which a program's performance can be judged. For example, when trying to determine death rates in a population, one must first know the normal death rate to determine whether mortality in the target population is abnormally high. In this case, relief authorities would obtain reference data on normal mortality among the population and compare it to the rates currently being experienced. The death rate in a population should not exceed the normal rate. If the normal rate is not known, the international reference figure of 1.0 per 10,000 per day may be used.

Standards are used as targets for supplying food, water, and other basic human needs. For example, WHO has set emergency water-quantity standards at thirty liters per person per day. A more realistic standard for emergencies, however, is ten liters per person per day. While some people such as infants and small children require less, adults doing heavy work in warm environments require more. The average standard is a means of making sure the families' total supply needs are met. In addition to the water standard mentioned earlier, the three most important standards are: the number of calories for relief rations (2,250–2,500 kcal), the number of latrines per family (1), and the amount of space per person for emergency shelters (3.5 square meters).

Indicators are aspects of a situation that can be monitored to give evidence of the overall situation, changes, or trends. Indicators are most often used in public health. For example, a reported increase in infant mortality could be a result of disease, starvation, or contaminated water. By cross-checking food consumption at the family level, water quality at distribution points, and diseases reported to aid stations or clinics, a more accurate picture of health and nutrition among the population can be gained. Thus, it is important to know which indicators to examine as points of entry in each sector.

The Importance of Credibility

A major objective of assessment planning is to establish its credibility. The assessment must be thorough and provide information in such a way that it reduces the necessity for other agencies or personnel to conduct their own assessments. In reality, few agencies accept the assessments of others. Most agencies want to conduct their own assessments to confirm what others have said. To some extent, this duplication can serve as a means of verification. But if an assessment is well planned, if the methodologies and procedures used provide an objective, clear, concise, and rapid picture of the situation, and if the assessment report describes the information-gathering techniques, procedures, and standards, the need for verification and follow-up assessments can be substantially reduced.

Detailed and overly sophisticated survey techniques can yield useful information for long-term planning but are usually of limited value for emergency assessment. The time required for data processing and interpretation can take longer than the time available for planning an emergency response. For this reason, assessments should be used to verify or refute the assumption on which an immediate response is made.

People must be consulted. Community social structures and re-sponses to the situation should be reviewed to find out how to provide relief in culturally acceptable and supportive ways.

Assessment Priorities

In an emergency, certain lifesaving interventions must be made im-mediately and certain systems must be established before other options can be brought into play. These responses begin as soon as famine con-ditions are recognized and follow a prescribed pattern until on-site assessments prove beyond a doubt that a specific set of interventions is not required. The assessments should begin simultaneously. The infor-mation collected is used to verify the types of problems that are occurring and to modify and adjust the responses. Therefore, in the initial recon-naissance, the assessment must focus on the primary threats to life that are expected and determine whether resources are being applied or are available to address the expected problems.

Since malnutrition, measles, and diarrhea are the main causes of death during a famine, the first task is to determine the level of these three threats. This is done by calculating the mortality rates, identify-ing the prevalent diseases and their incidence, determining the nutritional status of the vulnerable groups, and determining the preva-lence of diarrhea.

An effective response supplies ample food, immunization against priority diseases, and diarrhea control. Each of these responses—food security, immunization, clean water, ORT, and sanitation—requires that certain programs and systems be established and each meet minimum standards.

Water and sanitation issues require consideration of the physical site where the refugees are living. Issues such as space, shelter, and flood protection may also require attention. The way food will be provided must be considered. Top priorities are work programs to provide in-come and food logistics, including transport, fuel, and storage. In addition, the medical program requires close examination of the logis-tics system for receiving, transporting, and storing vaccines, that is, the cold chain.

Selecting the Assessment Team

An assessment team should be made up of people qualified to evalu-ate and report on the priority areas. Three- or four-person teams can carry out comprehensive assessment. The following configurations could be used:

Summary of Immediate Assessment Priorities

Step 1. Assess:

- Daily death rates
- Prevalence of disease and morbidity rates
- Nutritional status
- Prevalence of diarrhea

Step 2. Assess the food situation, including:

- The availability of staple grains, including:
  - Quantity
  - Quality
  - Cost
  - Affordability to poor
  - Geographic extent of the food-problem area
  - Local agricultural conditions
- Food-assistance programs, especially:
  - Methodology
  - System of enrollment and monitoring
  - Outreach

Step 3. Assess health programs, especially:

- Measles immunizations
- Integrity of the cold chain
- Record keeping (surveillance)
- Diarrhea-control program (oral rehydration)

Step 4. Assess water and sanitation programs, including:

- Amount of water supplied
- Quality of water
- Type of latrines in use
- Personal-hygiene habits of people

Step 5. Assess the logistics system, including:

- Availability and suitability of transport
- Availability of fuel
- Storage space in logistics system
- Availability of grain-milling facilities

Step 6. Identify labor-intensive, income-generating projects that can be started quickly.

Step 7. Assess potential for alternative food-security programs (cash for work and food for work).

Team Configurations

FUNCTION	PROFESSION
THREE-PERSON TEAM	
Health and nutrition	Nurse-nutritionist or physician
Water, sanitation, shelter	Engineer or planner
Logistics	Logistician
FOUR-PERSON TEAM	
Health and diarrhea	Nurse or physician
Nutrition and feeding	Nurse-nutritionist, dietician
Water, sanitation, shelter	Engineer or planner
Logistics	Logistician

13 | *Operational Issues*

Introduction

Throughout famine-relief operations, agencies will experience a variety of issues that slow progress or confuse the situation. These are common, and understanding them can provide some help in overcoming them.

Political Constraints

Assisting famine victims in the midst of a conflict is one of the most politically sensitive activities that relief agencies carry out. In cases where the government is one of the parties in a civil conflict, agencies are often placed in the difficult position of having to deal with government authorities who are unwilling or hesitant to provide assistance to people whom they consider enemies. In many cases, government actions or policies may be root causes of the conflict.

Relief agencies must often provide assistance from the government's side of the lines, and this can lead to charges they are not neutral. This is especially a problem when NGOs are operating as part of a broad UN operation. Many liberation groups mistrust the UN, because they often work with the permission of the host government. However, in reality, the majority of assistance provided to famine victims in conflicts is delivered from the government's side, since most people displaced by the famine and fighting tend to migrate to government-controlled areas. This occurs for a variety of reasons—people tend to follow normal migration routes, use family ties, and stay in areas where their language is spoken. The main reason, however, is they move toward the most viable economies, where the best opportunities for jobs are found. Migration is as much an economic-survival strategy as flight from conflict. The displaced must earn a living. Since they cannot rely on international relief, they must go where the economy is functioning. Chapter 14 is devoted to a more extensive discussion of the special conditions that pertain to famine operations during conflicts.

While the majority of political issues affecting famine response since 1975 have been related to conflict, some political issues in societies nominally at peace will also affect that response. Relief agencies often find that some populations are difficult to reach or that the government has placed obstacles in the way of serving certain populations. A politically instituted famine may have been used to ethnically cleanse areas or as a weapon against groups perceived as subversive. This occurred, for example, in Biafra in 1969. And the Sudanese government has been accused of indirectly withholding food from groups associated with government rebels.

Logistical Difficulties

It is often difficult to reach famine victims with assistance. In many cases, they reside in remote areas, where access is difficult and transportation may be poor. The topography may be rugged, and seasonable rains may make surface transportation hazardous and difficult. In conflict zones, security conditions may prohibit or severely restrict travel. In areas adjacent to conflict zones, security conditions may be marginal at best, especially for the displaced.

In these situations, full attention must be given to advance planning. It will often be necessary to stockpile supplies in or near the areas where people are going, so that shortages do not occur during times when these regions are isolated by conflict or climatic conditions.

In some cases, relief agencies may have to rely on extraordinary means of transport. Aircraft may have to supply garrison towns, and on-site management may also require the use of small planes to move quickly over vast areas, where needs can change instantaneously. Emergency operations are often said to require planning in three dimensions: air, land, and sea. However, operations planners should be aware that long-range relief operations, especially when aircraft are involved, are extremely expensive. Emphasis should be placed on procuring as many relief supplies as possible from local or nearby sources. It is often possible to use a broad range of local-market interventions that have the same result as large amounts of relief supplies brought from outside the affected area. (See Chapter 7.)

Structural Problems in the Relief System

Many humanitarian workers talk about the international relief system. However, no unified system exists. Rather, there are a variety of organizations that provide different types of assistance at different levels. They band together formally or informally as necessary. Some organizations act in the capacity of fundraisers and donors. Some provide funds directly to the famine victims. And others fund local agencies.

Within this ad hoc structure, there are many difficulties. NGOs are the primary operating agencies. While many have a wide range of capabilities, most specialize in a limited number of services. Many of the most important technical fields where lives can be saved are routinely overlooked. For example, only a handful of agencies have the capability of providing water and sanitation. Few agencies are experienced in setting up and maintaining the food-logistics systems required for providing massive food aid, and within the international community, no agency is specifically tasked with providing protection or security to the displaced.

Because of these structural deficiencies in the relief system, responses in critical areas are often ad hoc and uncoordinated. Added to this is the fact the international assistance system is vastly overstretched. Needs have grown beyond its ability to meet all requirements. Experienced personnel are often transferred from one operation to another before their original assignments are completed. While the agencies need to build up cadres of emergency-management personnel, the inconsistent nature of emergencies and the funding patterns of relief agencies preclude such measures.

Dealing with Food Shortages

Relief agencies or governments are often faced with situations where shortages of food supplies cause deaths. In these situations, the person in charge must decide quickly how to equitably distribute the available foods and keep deaths to an absolute minimum.

Relief administrators have three choices. They can:

- Give a fixed percent of the population a full ration and accept the resultant mortality
- Uniformly reduce the rations by a fixed percent
- Reallocate food according to need

In the first method, the food available is determined, and rations are sufficient to feed X percent of the population at normal levels. That percentage will receive the normal intake; the rest of the population will receive nothing. This is shown in Figure 13–1 below. For example, if there is a 20 percent shortfall in food, 80 percent of the population will receive adequate nutrition, and 20 percent will die (Manetsch 1981).

In the second method, the authorities supply a reduced ration to all people. This strategy is referred to as *hard rationing.*

In the third method, called *fair-share strategy,* food is distributed throughout the population according to need. Adjustments are made for such individual differences in requirements as size, work, age, sex, and pregnancy. If the total amount of food available is only a percentage of the normal requirement, all people will receive a reduction equal to that percentage of their normal food ration.

Each strategy will result in significantly different patterns of survival rates as shown in Figure 13–1, which is a comparison of the hard-rationing and fair-share techniques and their effect on survival.

To understand the graph, let us look at an example. Suppose for a given population, there is enough food to feed 99 percent of the people at a normal rate on a continuing basis. In the first strategy, 1 percent of the people would not receive enough food to survive. Yet if we were to reduce everyone's ration by only 1 percent, as in the hard-rationing strategy, all would probably survive if the food distribution were equitable.

At the other extreme, suppose we have a food shortage of 99 percent, and only 1 percent of the food supply is available to feed the same population. In this case, the survival rate would be 1 percent on the first distribution strategy, while 100 percent of the people would die using hard rationing or a fair-share distribution.

Comparison of these two curves on the graph suggests fair-share distribution can result in higher survival rates in a number of cases, but beyond a certain point, that strategy would result in a higher percentage of deaths. In our examples, that point occurs at the 50 percent level. In actual practice, where that point occurs is determined by many extraneous factors, including the amount of food being supplied, the supply mechanisms employed, and the planned oversupply allowance for children built into most relief-rationing schemes. Generally, the crossover point is at about the 40 percent shortage level.

Additional strategies for stretching food supplies include:

- *Better Targeting.* This can be accomplished by using more accurate recipient-targeting methods (which include weight-for-height measurements) for selecting families. Some food requirements in some areas could be reduced by 10 to 20 percent, if the agency received more accurate data on the needs of individual families.

- *Using Nutritional Status for Issuing Food Rations.* This approach can be used with nutrition-based feeding programs. If food supplies are scarce, the authorities can use a person's nutritional status as a means of determining how much food a family should be given. The program would provide full rations to families until children (who are used for monitoring overall nutritional status) have reached 90 to 100 percent of the weight-for-height standards for three months. At that point,

Figure 13–1

Comparison of Two Strategies for Food Distribution
and Their Effect on Survival

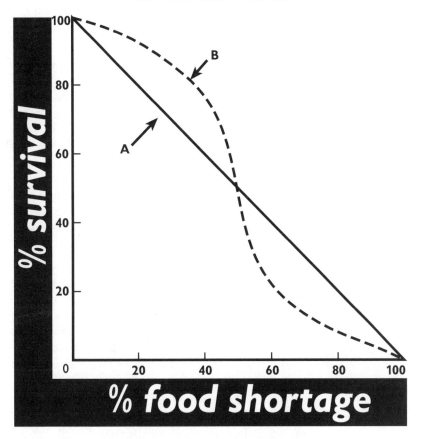

A: "Enough or nothing" distribution strategy
B: "Fair share" distribution strategy

rations could be reduced ten percent per month until the allocation is seventy percent of the full ration. If children show no further deterioration at that time, rations could be reduced to fifty percent for an additional three months. If no deterioration in the child's nutritional state occurs, he or she could be phased out of the program.

This approach is based on the following assumptions: (1) family food needs are not constant and change over time; (2)

while a family is receiving food, changes will occur in the overall food supply; and (3) food serves as income support, allowing the family to build up small cash reserves to be used to buy food to supplement the ration. Except in cases where severe agricultural constraints continue, relief agencies are not doing their job in the famine-recovery stage if food has to be supplied to the same family for more than six months.

- *Reducing Rations in Areas of Major Improvements in Food Production or Only Marginal Deficits.* Since famines shift geographically, it will probably be necessary to shift the assistance program to meet needs. If famine indicators are monitored monthly, it should be possible to detect the passage of acute famine conditions and begin reducing rations. As the price of food declines and people regain the ability to purchase food, rations can be gradually reduced to 70 to 75 percent of the normal amount. Continuing to give full food rations could have a negative effect on local-market prices in recovering regions and impede production. Food in these areas should be phased out as soon as practical and be sent to other places.

- *Reducing or Halting Food Distribution After Harvest.* Some food is produced even in the worst famines. When those crops are harvested, food distribution should be cut back or even temporarily halted for one to three months. The period of suspension can be adjusted based upon the amount harvested. This would allow the normal market to function as usual and would ensure that food distribution would not have an adverse impact on those areas where limited recovery is taking place.

- *Discharging Healthy People from the Rolls.* In many instances, people are kept in feeding programs or continue to receive assistance long after they have been nutritionally rehabilitated. When food supplies are scarce, program administrators should closely monitor people in the program and discharge healthy patients as soon as they have recovered. Those who are discharged can then be enrolled in income-support projects such as cash for work and food for work.

All the above strategies for stretching food depend upon strict nutritional surveillance and the monitoring of all communities in the program. The more accurate weight-for-height measuring needs to be used in these strategies.

Program staff should be alert for the problem of *rotating beneficiaries.* This occurs when people who have been nutritionally rehabilitated are phased out of the program too soon or without adequate means for maintaining their nutritional status. After leaving the program, they quickly deteriorate, and several months later require readmission.

Food-selection Issues

Cultural Acceptability

Famine victims often find donated foods are not suitable or desirable. This is a real and unpleasant aspect of food aid. Relief workers have reported on numerous occasions that foods have been refused, because they did not fit into existing dietary patterns. Although people who desperately need food sometimes accept unfamiliar products for a short time, they are more likely to reject food outright, even in states of severe malnutrition. In addition, the diseases that often accompany famines may further reduce the willingness of a community to eat unfamiliar foods. In some cases, unfamiliar foods can lead to diarrhea, which further complicates the human body's ability to respond to a feeding routine.

On several occasions, foods were first refused, then accepted, and then rejected again. These experiences usually occur after the first energy needs have been satisfied during a long-term food-relief program. When this pattern exists, however, it prevents total nutritional recovery and can result in large numbers of people hovering on the borderline of starvation.

To help food donors select the appropriate foods during a food emergency, the Food and Agricultural Organisation has prepared a provisional list of foods eaten in a number of countries. This report, titled "List of Major Foods Consumed in Selected Countries," is available from FAO in Rome from the Food Policy and Nutrition Division. It should be in every relief worker's reference library.

Mixing Foods to Balance Diets

A growing concern among relief nutritionists is the lack of balanced diets in feeding programs. For emergencies, food baskets should include a grain, a source of protein, and oil. But individuals also need a good mix of vitamins and minerals. In many areas, children do not receive enough Vitamin A and have problems with their eyes as a result. In a number of recent operations, scurvy, a disease that results from Vitamin C deficiency, has been seen in relief-camp populations. Pellagra, a niacin deficiency, has shown up in corn-consuming populations when lime has not been used to break down the outer shell of the corn's kernels. And in one camp in Thailand, beriberi broke out, because people had not received adequate supplies of Vitamin B, which is usually obtained from eating green leafy vegetables.

The diets of most societies have evolved over many years of practice and have some degree of nutritional balance, even the most basic ones. What people often do not receive nutritionally from the main staples comes from condiments and spices. A practical way to start planning a diet for famine victims is to examine people's normal eating patterns and try to build around them.

Boredom with Diets

Relief diets—especially those without spices—are often boring. In some refugee camps in Sudan in 1985, people were given a simple meal of bread, oil, and pulses (beans, peas, and other legumes) for months on end. Relief agencies reported many people lost interest in eating. Famine workers observed the same phenomenon in Ethiopia in 1974.

The best solution is to vary the diet, adding a different mix of vegetables and fruits as often as possible. But if food supplies are limited, providing a variety of spices may be the best short-term solution. That way, at least the taste of the food varies. In the Ethiopian case, relief workers distributed a local spice called *burpali*. Spices and condiments are rarely in short supply and can be readily purchased in local markets.

Dependency Concerns

Relief-program designers should be alert to the possibility that long-term food aid might foster dependencies that could ultimately lead to greater hardships for famine victims. Some agencies believe relief efforts should switch from dry-ration distribution to food for work or similar mechanisms to reduce the likelihood that dependencies will be created. Another way is to close out all food-distribution programs and switch to a variety of cash for work and cash-based development assistance. Special emphasis can be given to promoting agricultural recovery and stimulating food production.

There are two types of dependencies associated with food aid: perceived and situational.

Perceived dependency is an attitude. It can result from apathy, lethargy, frustration, and, commonly, paternalism. Development agencies are most concerned about the latter two, frustration and paternalism. They often result from programs that last a long time, have little input from victims, and continuously provide free goods and services. The victims often find it more convenient not to work. It is easier to receive food than to work to produce the food that would remove them from the distribution rolls. Perceived-dependency syndrome exists when disaster victims refuse to participate in self-help activities, when they demand that they be given more, or when they will not participate in food for work or similar programs.

While this behavior is frustrating for relief-agency personnel, it is not too serious. It may indicate that an excess of food aid is going into the community or that some people on the food rolls could be excluded. It usually is a sign that people are taking advantage of a program or the benevolence of the donors rather than that a true dependency exists.

Situational dependency is an economic condition in which forces created by the relief program have disrupted local economies and food-production cycles. Situational dependency should be of far more concern to relief agencies. Three types of dependencies can be created: *individual dependency, local economic dependency,* and *national agricultural dependency.*

Individual dependencies occur when people are able to obtain more food from relief programs than they can get by working at their normal endeavors. There are hidden disincentives in relief projects that tend to discourage food production. If a farmer can earn more food in a food-for-work project than he can on his fields and if the work project requires him to spend most of his time on the project, he is unlikely to till his fields. If this occurs during the planting season, he could become dependent on food aid for the remainder of the year. For this reason, salaries in cash- and food-for-work programs should be lower than normal wages. If they are equal to or higher than normal, the relief agency may find itself the principal employer in the area.

Local economic dependency is a far more serious situation. It occurs when food-aid distributions affect the agro-economy of a community. If large amounts of food aid are distributed throughout the year, local farmers may find a depressed market after harvest. If they cannot sell enough food to recoup their investment or buy seeds for the following year, they may be compelled to seek work away from their farms. This results in less production the following year and a further lowering of the overall harvest level. When this occurs, more people may be forced onto the relief rolls. A cycle of dependency can eventually develop.

National food dependency occurs when the amount of food being imported brings supplies in the country up to a level that is greater than the amount normally grown nationwide. Even if that level is still less than the total food need, food prices nationwide may drop below the cost of production. This occurs because commercial food sales normally make up the difference between food production and total demand. If imported food continues too long, it may replace some of the commercial imports and lower prices, thereby creating a disincentive to local production. National dependencies are not usually the result of famine-assistance programs but of normal food-aid imports. They sometimes start in the aftermath of famine-assistance programs.

The following steps can help reduce the likelihood dependencies will be inadvertently created by food-aid programs.

- Careful targeting of food aid
- Using caution in establishing food-for-work programs
- Using a food store/coupon approach in lieu of food for work
- Phasing out food aid as quickly as possible whenever feasible. Experimental reduction of food aid linked to food production should be tried continually.

Women's Issues

The majority of adult famine victims are lactating and pregnant women and elderly people, and most are heads of households. In many programs, especially in conflict zones, women and children make up two-thirds to three-quarters of the population. Yet most relief programs have a distinct male bias. For example, many loan programs are less effective, because women are not eligible to apply. Other programs such as food for work are often predicated on males being the primary breadwinners.

Women's programs are increasingly recognized as an important part of any development program. Few go beyond handicraft projects or small cottage industries. No program of assistance for displaced people will succeed unless it is designed to involve women in decision making at all levels.

Women in Income-support Projects

Women make up half the rural work force and are involved in most agricultural activities. Their working hours tend to be much longer than those of their male counterparts—they are responsible for taking care of the family, working in the fields, helping with the livestock, collecting firewood and water, all in addition to maintaining the home. They frequently share the responsibility of bringing in an income. Because of the lack of technology, even the simplest tasks can be burdensome and time consuming, requiring great physical labor and limiting the woman's ability to participate in social and economic development. This results in an underuse of a productive sector of the population.

In planning income-support projects, consideration must be given to increasing women's participation. Projects should be designed so that women can continue their necessary daily activities at home. Activities should take place close to the home or village and should not require every participating woman to spend the entire day on the job. Hours should be flexible, so women with dependent households can attend to other responsibilities. Projects should also introduce new technologies to help women reduce their daily burdens. For example, rural women are traditionally responsible for fetching firewood. This can consume several hours each day, especially when people are living in periurban settings or refugee camps: nearby trees can be quickly depleted, and people may have to go farther each day to find wood. Introduction of more efficient wood-burning stoves would make the task easier and help slow environmental degradation. This said, some recent evidence points to the value of interior smoke in reducing insect populations in living areas.

Women can participate in anything men can do so long as their tasks do not involve heavy labor. The following summarizes the considerations for projects that will facilitate women's participation:

- They should be close-to-home activities
- They should be in accessible areas
- They should require only a few hours a day
- They should not involve unusually heavy labor
- A child-care program should be established, so mothers can leave their infants and young children in proper care

Types of activities appropriate for women include:

- Earth-moving projects in which dirt and gravel need to be carried. This includes terracing, road building, and clearing sites for construction projects.
- Tree planting in reforestation projects
- Clearing light brush for farmland or reforestation projects
- Maintaining windbreaks
- Most aspects of small building projects including clinics, outpatient facilities, mother-child health centers, schools, and community centers. Women can be involved in tasks ranging from ground clearing to roofing.
- Helping with the production of cooperatively produced or marketed crops, such as roasting and turning coffee beans or winnowing and thrashing wheat
- Operation and maintenance of day-care centers and involvement in food-distribution center activities (Intertect 1985)

Preserving People's Dignity During Food Relief

Dependency is a problem of the spirit more than anything. Receiving free food for long periods can rob people of their dignity and self-esteem. To reduce this problem, at least two approaches should be considered.

The first provides work that results in either cash, script, coupons, or credit to purchase food. In these cases, food sales should be permitted.

A second approach allows people to use cash or bartered materials for the food they receive. The contributions should not be considered payment for food but a voluntary contribution. Nor is it a true hardship for those people who can make the offering. Contributions help people preserve their dignity when they are facing pressures that could create perceived dependencies.

General Operational Concerns

Coordination

Many of the difficulties in relief operations arise, because national and international groups have not coordinated their efforts or worked effectively with local governments (Cox 1981). There are several reasons coordination is difficult. First, agencies rarely agree on what approach is the most effective to use in a situation. This is particularly a problem when new, inexperienced agencies come onto the scene. And second, there are few internationally recognized standards for programs. Even agencies involved in feeding programs do not agree on the services to be offered and the levels of assistance to be given. If the local government or UN does not set standards, there is no basis for coordination.

One of the most important actions that need to be taken early in an emergency is the joint development of program standards, standard-operating procedures, and mutually acceptable protocol or programs.

Staffing

An effective relief organization requires more than food and medical personnel. It must also have technicians to conduct assessments and monitor all aspects of the famine; public-health workers, especially those trained in epidemiology, to treat and prevent famine-associated disease; logistics personnel to handle the acquisition, transport, and distribution of materials; business and economic specialists to deal with financial matters and give advice on the integration of the relief activities into the local economy; and liaison personnel to mesh relief work with the local civil authority. An effective operation requires that relief workers with little knowledge of the local scene be brought in and trained quickly, that a large variety of food and other materials be mobilized from distant sources, and that a fleet of vehicles of some size and diversity be deployed and maintained.

14 | Famine Operations During Conflicts

Denying food to one's foes to try to weaken their resistance is a tactic as old as war itself. The sieges of the Middle Ages, for example, were often characterized by attempts to starve people inside walled cities into submission. In the civil and separatist conflicts of the latter part of the twentieth century, withholding food has become even more widespread as a tactic. And when it comes from a government trying to starve segments of its own people, as it often does, it has unprecedented viciousness. In addition, today's warriors intentionally target civilians in far greater numbers than in, say, World War I.

It is perplexing why the tactic is still used after all these centuries. Ultimately, it is a failure. All the great military strategists, from Carl von Clausewitz to North Vietnamese General Vo Nyien Giap, have said that making war on the civil population solidifies the opposition and stiffens its resolve. Few, if any, wars have been won by starving the enemy's civilians. Those bearing arms will always be the first to receive food. Even the indirect effects, such as famine's impact on morale, are greatly overestimated. During the U.S. Civil War, enlistments in the Confederate Army increased so much during William Tecumseh Sherman's scorched-earth campaign, they more than compensated for desertions. In some cases, the enlistees wanted revenge. In most, they knew the Army was the only source of a good meal.

In spite of what military history has shown, relief officials constantly have to provide famine assistance during today's proliferating conflicts. For the most part, the politics of the moment—as well as the military situation—dictate the strategies for famine assistance. In recent years, however, a number of approaches have been developed that might be applied in other situations. Before discussing them, a brief look at some of the recurring patterns and consequences of war that have an impact on relief operations is called for.

From an operational point of view, the two most important constraints created by war are the collapse of the normal food-marketing system and the massive displacement of the civil population. In their dislocation, people may have been forced to abandon their convertible assets, hastening the onset of famine conditions. Their inability to buy food and the collapse of the market system mean an artificial food-distribution system may have been set up. This does not rule out income-support programs, however. In fact, food will still be available within the conflict zone but at abnormally high prices, especially if wholesale merchants are hoarding it.

Displacement complicates relief operations in many ways. People may migrate within the conflict zone. They may move to areas outside the zone but within the country. Or they may seek asylum in a neighboring country. Each migration pattern requires a different set of approaches, and each approach, if successful, will influence what options people may seek when they are displaced.

The fact that displacement rarely follows a predicable pattern makes it difficult to strategically place counterfamine resources. Pockets of need may develop over a wide geographic area and may shift dramatically as people are forced to flee. Combatants may destroy or confiscate food, creating instant food shortages that cannot be foreseen. In this environment, the need for a strong and flexible logistics system is paramount.

People tend to congregate in relief camps. And the failure of relief agencies to find alternative living situations for them poses other problems for supplying emergency aid. High-density camps require massive infrastructures be set up to provide basic services, such as water, sanitary services, and shelter. The term camp is a misnomer. It is a community with the same needs as a town. There are alternatives, but few agencies use them.

In many cases, displaced people migrate to urban centers in search of jobs. They usually form or move into squatter settlements on the periphery of towns and cities. Obtaining food is less of a problem if the city is outside the conflict zone. People can find work and procure food in most urban areas. Food deficiencies will occur periodically, but the problem is usually hunger, not famine. People migrating to cities within the conflict zone are another matter, especially when they go to garrison towns surrounded by opposing forces. In this case, famine conditions usually exist in the settlements of the displaced.

Crowding in both camps and settlements makes another problem worse: communicable disease. As we have seen, when people are nutritionally weak, it is difficult for them to resist disease. If a disease breaks out in these dense settlements with poor sanitation, it can spread rapidly.

The movement of food is the major factor determining the success of a famine-relief operation during a war. As we have noted, logistics is complex, costly, and slow—and, in war, it is even more so. Adjusting and redirecting food supplies to meet changing needs can be a frustrating exercise and is often a no-win situation. For this reason, agencies should be alert to alternative ways of freeing food supplies in and adjacent to the conflict zone. They should constantly seek alternatives to artificial distribution systems. One should never assume there is no food available—experience shows there will always be some, even in the worst situations. The problem is how to get it released and flowing into the hands of people who need it.

There are three situations that relief agencies commonly face:

- Operating at the periphery of the conflict zone on the government's side
- Operating from the periphery on the government's side, sending relief across the lines (cross-line operations)
- Operating from a neighboring country into rebel-held areas (cross-border operations)

Operations on the Periphery

Relief operations on the periphery of a conflict zone are usually focused on assisting people who have been forced out of an area due to fighting. Typically, feeding centers and temporary camps are set up in the first safe place the displaced stop after leaving the conflict zone. In many cases, people are in terrible shape: They may be severely malnourished, sick, exhausted from their evacuation, and traumatized by attacks upon them during their journey. And in some cases, they may have contracted diseases endemic to the area they passed through but for which they had no resistance. Typically, large numbers of people will arrive without any visible assets, and families may be separated from or have lost family members.

In these conditions, emergency assistance and relief are required. Typically, large percentages of people will accumulate around a health post, a water location, or other rallying point, and a camp will evolve. Needs include food, nutritional rehabilitation, medical and public-health assistance, water, and possibly protection. Relief agencies can expect the majority of the displaced in the worst condition to congregate in relief camps.

Operationally, the emergency phase will last as long as there are new arrivals and malnutrition, morbidity, and mortality rates are above normal. From the migrants' point of view, however, the emergency phase lasts either until they can be assured their families can live on the assistance being provided or they have accumulated enough resources to move on to an area where they can find steady employment.

In the initial stages of a conflict, the early arrivals may be able to find employment in nearby towns or on local farms, especially if farmers have a tradition of employing migrant labor or establishing temporary sharecropping relationships. But soon, all openings will be taken. The job market will be saturated and the wage scale sufficiently depressed, so that subsequent arrivals must move outward in search of income. Increasing the availability of jobs in the area may be a viable strategy for reducing the burden on relief agencies and for holding people in the area. This can be done by initiating cash-for-work projects or another of a variety of community-development programs.

Another strategy that has been used with some success is *paired villages*. In this approach, the nonresident population (the displaced or returnees) are formed into new villages that are then moved to and paired with existing villages inside the enclave. Relief agencies provide a range of assistance to help the outsiders integrate into the local economy in ways that are mutually beneficial to both communities. The ultimate objective is to achieve a symbiotic relationship.

The program should be carried out on a village-by-village basis. First, potential host villages are identified in areas where additional labor could increase agricultural or economic productivity. Leaders are then asked whether they would accept the establishment of a temporary settlement adjacent to their village. In return for accepting people, the host village is assured priority for development assistance.

When a village agrees to accept the newcomers, families are formed into groups according to their original village, area of origin, or ethnic group. Then they are taken to the new site, where they receive temporary food rations, materials to build shelters, and assistance designed to help them integrate into the community and economy.

At the same time, relief agencies provide comprehensive assistance designed to help the two communities coexist. The first activity usually involves upgrading or expanding water supplies, then enlarging health services. Public-works projects to improve the local environment, agricultural extension, rehabilitation assistance, and construction of schools or other facilities come next—all in accordance with priorities established with the local leaders.

This approach has many advantages for both people and relief agencies. There are, however, some potentially serious implications that should be recognized, not the least of which is the likelihood that the host village will exploit the temporary residents (Cuny 1988). The factors likely to determine the success of the approach are:

- The selection of villages that can absorb the new population and can accept the newcomers with a minimum of intercultural conflict
- Capacity of the local economy to absorb new workers
- The degree to which the host population remains receptive to the outsiders, which often depends on how much aid they receive
- The degree to which the nonresidents' former village life-style and social systems can be maintained

On the whole, however, paired settlements are workable strategies.

Cross-line Operations

Cross-line Feeding Programs

In cases where battle lines are well defined and it is difficult for people to cross between opposing forces, it may be possible to negotiate a cross-line feeding program. An example of such a program is the Northern Initiative that was set up in Ethiopia in 1985 to feed famine victims in the conflict zones in the north. Several large NGOs were selected to operate the program on behalf of the donors—they were perceived by all parties as being neutral. One part of the program, operated by Catholic Relief Services (CRS) in Eritrea, is representative.

The long war in the north, which began in the 1960s, had made progressively deeper cuts in the area's food production. To make up for these shortages, a number of relief agencies began a cross-border supply operation from neighboring Sudan. (See section below.)

As the Ethiopian famine developed in the early 1980s, major donors began to consider increasing the level of support for the cross-border program. The program's potential to meet increasing needs was limited, however, by logistics problems and the tonnage that could be delivered. Furthermore, the Ethiopian military periodically threatened to cut off the operation. It was not too great a threat at the time: the operation's small scale made the convoys difficult to intercept. But the program could become more important if the operation grew in size and consequently became more visible.

By late 1984, the famine in northern Ethiopia had reached such proportions that hundreds of thousands of people were streaming into Sudan, and millions more were estimated to be in critical situations in the rebel-held areas. People had two choices: moving into relief centers in the government-held areas or moving westward into Sudan in search of food. Both options were seen as disruptive. As long as the refugees or displaced people were being fed in relief centers, away from their villages, chances for agricultural recovery were minimal.

In response to the situation, a number of relief agencies sought permission to initiate feeding programs from bases in government-controlled areas. After much negotiation, the Ethiopian government agreed to a program that would place food at the forward edge of the government lines. Local villagers would be allowed to pass through the lines to collect food and return to their communities. It was hoped this program could feed a significant portion of the famine victims and keep people from becoming refugees or displaced people.

The CRS program, which was carried out through the Ethiopian Catholic Secretariat, worked as follows: Local priests were permitted to cross the government lines to visit villages in the famine zone and estimate needs. Village elders were asked to identify people in the villages who needed food and to prepare lists. The lists were submitted to CRS logisticians, who then prepared estimates of the monthly tonnages required. Based on these estimates, CRS trucks delivered food to churches located at the edge of the conflict zone. On appointed dates, church workers then took food stocks to designated sites that government troops withdrew from. Then village representatives came through the lines to collect and transport food to their villages. In the villages, elders were responsible for ensuring food reached the intended beneficiaries.

Priests were also permitted to cross the lines to monitor distribution in the villages, although monitoring was always problematic. At the height of operations, CRS was distributing about 3,000 metric tons of food per month in Eritrea for a target population of 200,000 people.

The Northern Initiative was not the only way food was provided in the rebel-held areas. In addition, the cross-border operation from Sudan delivered 3,500 tons per month, an airlift to several garrison towns supplied 4,800 metric tons, airdrops from low-flying transports delivered 1,500 metric tons, and an International Committee of the Red Cross (ICRC) food-supply operation provided 2,600 tons. Therefore, it is difficult to accurately judge the overall impact of the program. However, it must be conceded the Northern Initiative was an important factor in increasing food supplies in the famine zone.

The most serious constraint on a cross-line program is the difficulty in monitoring food distribution. In the CRS program, the priests who crossed the lines had neither the time nor the resources to interview more than a few selected families or observe the distributions as they occurred. It would have been difficult for them to detect abuses and food diversion, unless the practices were widespread. Therefore, intentional diversion, withholding of supplies, or outright thefts could affect distribution at the village level. Even more probable, unintentional distribution problems could have been caused by a combination of inaccurate weighing or measuring of food as it was distributed and poor record keeping on the part of those responsible for distributing food.

There is a major logistical constraint on this type of program: the areas from which food is distributed must usually be government controlled. In more rugged terrain, the maximum distance people are willing to travel for food is approximately a three-day journey. In areas where governments control the roads, there may be pockets where people are not receiving food, because the distances are too far.

Market-based Approaches (Spillover Strategies)

In some cases, it may be possible to increase food supplies in the markets on the edge of the conflict zone. As supplies increase, prices decrease. At some point, traders from the famine zone or those who can pass safely through the lines will purchase food and transport it back into rebel-held territory. This approach, called *spillover*, requires some degree of caution when selling food in the peripheral markets. There is always the danger that prices could be depressed so low that they undercut local farmers. When purchasing power is extremely low in the target area, it sometimes must be coupled with income generation in the villages.

One way to protect local producers is to set up special arrangements for traders who are willing to run the risks of carrying food into the conflict zone. This can be done by selling to designated traders from special supplies set aside for this purpose. Prices would be low enough to make it worth the risks.

Relief Strategies in Rebel-held Areas

In many countries, rebels effectively control the countryside. Government troops venture out of their garrisons, usually in larger rural towns, only sporadically. In these cases, a number of initiatives can be taken to provide famine relief. The most common are shipping food across the border to distribute to famine victims and procuring grain from suppliers in or adjacent to the famine zone and redistributing it via relief programs or market sales. The first program is called *cross-border* relief and the second *internal purchase*. Once food arrives in the famine zone, how it is distributed depends on the degree of security in the area. If the area is relatively secure, food-distribution patterns are similar to those used in regions outside the conflict zone.

Cross-border Relief

In some cases, it may be possible and desirable to deliver food into the heart of the conflict zone. The most common approaches are: open-roads programs, where relief agencies negotiate an agreement with both sides to permit convoys to cross the border on designated routes to safe distribution points; cross-border operations, where food is trucked surreptitiously, usually at night from a neighboring country, to distribution points held by the insurgents; and air-supply operations, where food is flown into the famine zone, overflying contested areas. Since the first two rely on ground transport, they are the preferred methods—they are the most effective and least costly. But the more food travels, the greater the opportunity for criminals, warlords, or militia to divert it for their own use.

Perhaps two of the most successful examples of cross-border operations carried food from Sudan into Eritrea and Tigray in northern Ethiopia. Each operated effectively for many years, and they were cited as one of the reasons that relatively few Ethiopian refugees came to Sudan during the 1984–85 Ethiopian famine. More importantly, they were one of the reasons major famine conditions did not break out again in 1987.

The operation was supported by a consortium of agencies with offices in Sudan and Europe that raised funds, procured food, and monitored the program on behalf of the donors. All transport and delivery was handled by indigenous relief organizations affiliated with the rebels. The overall strategy was to provide food to people in their villages, so they would not have to relocate in times of severe shortage. In

1988, transport capacity for the Tigrayan operation averaged 5,000 metric tons per month. Food supplies were transported across the border by vehicles of the Relief Society of Tigray (REST) from storage facilities in Sudan. There was a central transit facility approximately 100 kilometers from the border. From there, routes branched out to ten distribution sites in western and central Tigray. The farthest point in the system was approximately 500 kilometers from the border. With this operation, almost 400,000 people received food on an emergency basis.

The primary constraint on cross-border operations is security. When operating over wide areas, it may be possible to conceal the routes and make deliveries without much danger. In small, confined areas, however, the chances of being detected increase, and losses can be high enough to force alternative approaches.

The delivery of food should be only one part of an agency's assistance program. The cross-border operation in Tigray was, at its best, only one of several approaches being used—cash distribution to families with vulnerable children and internal purchases were carried out simultaneously.

Internal food-delivery projects require donors to make a major leap of faith: most assistance requires support and sometimes participation by the insurgents. Nonetheless, it is possible to establish some degree of accountability. For example, Biafran authorities in the Nigerian civil war (1967–70) did an excellent job distributing the aid flown in. Likewise, most donors have been satisfied with the way the Eritrean and Tigrayan groups distributed food aid in northern Ethiopia.

Perhaps the most important question is: does the assistance reach the intended beneficiaries? The answer might seem straightforward—if the aid does not reach the beneficiaries, they'll move. But conflicts may prevent movement. For this reason, careful monitoring is necessary.

Agencies undertaking internal-delivery programs without government sanction must also be aware of the logistical difficulties. Private contractors may be reluctant to risk their own vehicles in such a situation. Therefore, the agency may have to buy and maintain a fleet of trucks. Because deliveries will be off main roads and often over difficult terrain, those vehicles must be rugged. And much time and attention will go into maintenance. Above all, the vehicles should be expendable—invariably some will be lost to hostile action, taken by rebel forces for their own use, or torn up by road conditions.

Agencies must also recognize that the food-aid efforts will, in the eyes of the government, put them on the side of the insurgents—humanitarian neutrality in a civil war is a distinctly Western concept, not necessarily welcome in the third world. If the agency has other relief or development programs in the country, the government may sharply curtail them when the agency begins to operate in rebel areas.

In spite of these problems, cross-border food deliveries are important. Providing food, directly or indirectly, helps keep people at home.

If access to food declines as a result of the conflict, displacement will increase and mortality will rise. Any strategy that can help reduce displacement is an important element in reducing the number of deaths.

Internal Purchase

In many situations, the purchase and distribution of internally available food reserves is a viable alternative to imported food aid. In most conflicts and famines, the amount of accessible food is far more than outsiders realize. Often cereals, pulses, and livestock may be available. Since famines are usually the result of market disturbances and conflicts disrupt normal marketing, food is often trapped in pockets where it cannot be sold or transported. In an internal-purchase program, a relief agency locates sources of supply, imports local currency to buy food, and then purchases and redistributes it, either by selling it at lower prices or giving it to relief agencies or committees in the famine or conflict zone to distribute through selective feeding or targeted food programs.

Internal purchase has many advantages. It is faster than importing food, is less costly, and can usually be managed by a few people working with local merchants and traders. Usually, once merchants start to release food they are hoarding, others will also start to sell, especially if the agency is reselling food to local vendors at low prices. Thus, the primary advantage is that it can help to reactivate the normal market system.

Food obtained through an internal-purchase operation is often more compatible with local tastes than imported foods. When food is sold, the proceeds can be used to buy more food or to support cash-for-work projects that give the poorest a chance to earn money to participate in the sales.

While the acquisition of internal food supplies is often more effective than external food aid, it is important to be sure that buying and distributing local food reserves does not significantly disrupt the local economy. For example, villages outside the famine zone may produce a surplus. However, if adjacent villages are producing at a marginal or subsistence level, the adjacent villagers may depend on that surplus for their own protection. Since famines shift geographically, it is important to carefully analyze food availability.

Operations in Border Enclaves

Another cross-border operation increasingly faced by relief organizations is support to people in border enclaves. Large numbers of civilians displaced by fighting often accumulate in enclaves along the border of a neighboring country. These groups may include a homogeneous ethnic or political group or may represent a variety of minorities, political factions, former soldiers, and other disparate groups. Some may cross the border to seek asylum as refugees, but in many cases, a larger number will stay in their own country, possibly slipping back and forth across the border to seek food and assistance.

Internal Purchase in Tigray: A Case Study

Providing relief food to 1.5 million people in Tigray province of northern Ethiopia was difficult because of the continuing insurgency as well as political and logistical problems. In November 1984, however, the Relief Society of Tigray determined that 25,000 metric tons of grain usually sold to Eritrean buyers or held in reserve by merchants was available in western Tigray. REST appealed to donors to provide currency to procure the grain for distribution to famine victims.

Donors were hesitant at first. Several were suspicious about the severity of the famine if food was available. Since REST was affiliated with the Tigray People's Liberation Front, the insurgents who controlled the area, the proposal required working outside government channels. Most donors were reluctant to give hard currency to buy food.

The cost of the grain was high, more than in Europe or the United States. It was feared, however, that food from abroad would not arrive in time to save lives. Thousands of people were preparing to migrate to Sudan or other areas, and starvation was already occurring in large areas of the region. Thus, the acquisition of available grains seemed a necessary intervention. With some hesitation, church agencies in Europe provided $200,000 for the first purchase.

Planning and implementation was primarily undertaken by REST, which identified the merchants, determined average prices, and supervised transportation, storage, and distribution of the grain. REST and a donor representative initially purchased what was necessary.

The purchase proceeded smoothly, though there were problems. Original plans called for the procurement of 10,000 metric tons of sorghum, which left a sizeable amount available for local needs and trade. However, during the time it took to convince donors to proceed, the available surplus dwindled to 3,000 metric tons and the price rose. The exchange of currency was difficult and cumbersome. Hard currency was sent to Sudan, drawn from the bank in cash, and transported to the border, where it was converted into *birr*, the Ethiopian currency. *Birr* was available only in small notes; hence, the bulk carried was considerable. As the program continued, the supply of notes dwindled and often delayed it.

Even with these problems, the program was rated an overall success in the short term. It was estimated that the internally purchased food arrived months earlier than imported food. Donors continued to support the program during periods of scarcity, and an efficient system of procurement developed. The long-term impact of the program, however, was unclear, since no one knew what role donor intervention played in the market economy.

Implementing an Internal Purchase Program

Step 1:   Assess whether food is available in the country to meet local needs.

Step 2:   Inform the local authorities that a feasibility study will be conducted for internal purchase.

Step 3:   Establish an assessment team.

Step 4:   Determine the amount of food available for purchase by assessing the gross surplus and subtracting the amount required for local needs and local trade.

Step 5:   Identify the implementing agency.

Step 6:   Assess the availability of local currency and the steps needed to convert hard currency into local currency.

Step 7:   Assess the availability and requirements for transportation, storage, and containers.

Step 8:   Determine the maximum contract size, identify local sellers, and develop a list of them and the location(s) and amount(s) of their supplies.

Step 9:   Evaluate the feasibility of the program by comparing the time and cost factors to those of importing food; assess the logistical needs of the operation.

Step 10:   Inform the local and/or national authorities of your intent to proceed; enlist their support for the currency exchange and obtain taxation information from them.

Step 11:   Proceed with the actual purchase:
- Determine the amount of food to be purchased
- Convert and transport the currency
- Prepare contracts
- Negotiate with sellers
- Develop, purchase, and distribute the plan
- Conduct the purchase

The reasons these people remain in their own country are mixed: Some stay, because they do not trust the government of the neighboring country. Some fear being put in refugee camps. Others may be waiting for members of their family, village, or group to catch up. And in some cases, armed factions operating in the area may restrain people.

There are several categories of people who may need assistance. They include:

- Refugees who have crossed the border into the neighboring country
- Displaced people who have congregated but not crossed the border—they are often found in a variety of spontaneous encampments along the border
- People who have been affected by the conflict deeper inside the

country but who have not fled their immediate areas
- Refugees who fled the country but quickly decided to return (called *ricochet repatriates*)
- Villagers who find it increasingly difficult to survive because of increased competition for resources in the enclave

Until recently, the conventional approach was to encourage the neighboring country to grant unrestricted asylum, so people could leave their country of origin and receive protection and assistance until they could be repatriated safely. However, current thought among relief practitioners holds that if the situation is safe enough for people to stay inside the enclave, it is usually desirable for most to do so. The determinants of whether this strategy should be pursued are:

- The degree of safety and security likely to exist during people's stay in the enclave and whether operations in the area will make the enclave a target
- Whether sufficient supplies can be delivered to support the population in the enclave (the displaced plus the host population)
- The degree of cooperation and flexibility that armed factions within the area extend to relief agencies

The reason this strategy is being increasingly advocated is straightforward: relief agencies usually have a freer hand in helping people in countries of origin, not refugees in host countries. Despite a variety of international conventions and protocols designed to promote assistance and protection, in reality, few host countries welcome refugees, and most are increasingly harsh in their treatment of them. The majority of refugees are placed in squalid camps without adequate food, water, or sanitary services. Recent comparisons of mortality among refugees and those who remain behind in conflict areas show that, in most cases, people have a better chance of survival in war zones. Refugees are restricted from working and face a long, debilitating existence where they are increasingly marginalized and disenfranchised. Relief agencies operating in border enclaves can often pursue a wider range of options to assist people and can help them attain a larger degree of self-sufficiency than would be possible in refugee camps. Furthermore, the government of the neighboring country can usually be persuaded to permit relief agencies to operate from the border and stage relief into the enclave—the government will overlook the issue of national sovereignty and all other legal issues to keep the refugees out.

Both the UN and ICRC are often unable to provide effective assistance or protection for people in enclaves, since their operations require permission from the host government. But that government is not likely to give its permission to foreign agencies to establish an international presence in areas outside its control. Thus, the task usually falls to NGOs, which are not constrained by international agreements like those that govern the UN. If the population is not too large and the major donors support their operations, NGOs can usually provide the services that are required.

Operations in enclaves usually require a multipronged approach:

- *Assistance to Refugees Who Have Crossed the Border.* This is necessary for humanitarian reasons as well as to keep the host country off the agencies' backs. Primary responsibility for assistance and protection of refugees in the country of asylum lies with the host government and UNHCR.

- *Assistance to Communities Impacted by the Influx of Refugees.* This is usually accomplished through a refugee-affected-areas program carried out by the UN, ICRC, and private relief agencies. This program has two purposes: (1) to equalize the amount of assistance being given in the border area, so resources are not drawn out of the enclave into the neighboring country and (2) to take the pressures off the host government, so it will give relief agencies more freedom to operate.

- *Assistance to Displaced People (and Returnees) Who Have Moved into the Enclaves.* Assistance is provided via a mix of cross-border relief programs. NGOs usually organize relief operations, possibly working with ICRC—though this is often not possible—or with UNICEF. UNICEF is one UN agency that can work in nongovernment-controlled areas, since its mandate gives it the right to work in any environment in which children are in danger. Food and relief supplies are staged across the border, using a combination of approaches, including:

  - Direct relief, where agencies take food and medical assistance across the border and deliver it to people

  - A take-away approach, where designated representatives of villages or other specific groups come to relief points along the border to pick up food to take back to their people

  - Market interventions, where food is sold to merchants to take back to village markets for resale. The proceeds of the sales, in local currency, are put back into the community via cash-for-work schemes, employment of public workers, and agriculture and livestock rehabilitation activities.

- *Assistance to Villages in the Enclave Affected by the Influx of Displaced People (and/or Returnees).* Villages in enclaves are affected not only by increased competition for resources such as water but may also be subjected to increased insecurity both from armed groups among the displaced as well as from attacks by the government or other combatants. They may also be cut off from their normal markets in their own country and the neighboring state, thus impoverishing people and increasing their vulnerability to food shortages. Because of these, it is important to tailor relief programs to include the resident population and meet a variety of needs. If this is not done, people may be displaced. Focusing on the resident community early in the assistance effort can also relieve many of the pressures that can quickly develop on the displaced population and help relief agencies obtain cooperation from local leaders.

As in all community-focused famine-mitigation activities, after a short period of relief operations, the focus should shift to longer-term, more development- and rehabilitation-style projects and activities. For example, schemes should be explored to provide farmers with small plots of land to work until they can return to their own land (called *alternative land leases*). All programs in the enclave should be designed so the people can operate them, with minimal intervention from relief agencies.

Some of the programs that can be undertaken in enclaves are:

- Market interventions
- Internal purchase
- Agricultural-inputs distribution
- Direct food relief (via cross-border food deliveries)
- Livestock interventions, including purchase and redistribution, market support, and veterinary services (vaccinations)
- Reentitlement (short-term employment, usually through cash-for-work projects)
- Rural water-system rehabilitation

Operations in border enclaves can often provide a workable alternative to asylum and can help the displaced temporarily live relatively productive lives in dignity and in an environment where they have more control over their own lives. If security and resources permit, refugees may be drawn back into the enclave through spontaneous repatriation. However, it must be recognized that security is paramount. If people feel threatened, they will quickly abandon the enclave and may seek refuge in a nearby country. Agencies working in enclaves should be prepared for sudden changes that could alter the nature of their work, increase or decrease their caseload, and possibly undo months of work. On the other hand, enclaves that remain calm can sometimes provide a basis for expanding the area of relative stability and can be a means of stimulating talks to resolve the conflict.

Operational Concerns in Conflict Zones

Any operation into rebel-held territory is likely to be fraught with problems, not the least of which is targeting and monitoring assistance. Income-support programs may be accused of providing cash that will eventually end up in the hands of the insurgents. Claims will be made that food aid will be skimmed off by fighters and not given to the intended people. In many cases, the militants will have already obtained the food they need, and the small amount of currency that would be skimmed off, especially if it is local currency, will have little value on the international arms market.

Dealing with Liberation Movements

A major constraint to helping people in rebel-held areas is the fact that organizations must deal with an antigovernment group. Officially, the UN can only do so with the concurrence of the government. This means that many opportunities to help famine victims are lost. In some cases, the government may agree to make limited contact with the insurgents. While the government may not be comfortable with these arrangements, there are advantages to them that it recognizes. With patience, it should be possible to establish a wide range of contacts, either directly or indirectly, with rebel groups even in the midst of intensive military campaigns. Over time, it may be possible to negotiate point-by-point agreements of what can and cannot be done in areas that rebels control or in which they are operating that will permit agencies to provide support in contested areas. It is important, however, that projects launched from the government side are not co-opted as pacification efforts or come to be viewed by the rebels as supporting pacification. The specific modalities of working with rebel groups or their supporters must be undertaken with extreme care, and every effort must be made to ensure all sides approve specific projects or activities.

Food-distribution Problems in Conflict Zones

When relief workers distribute food during a conflict without supervision, a number of problems are likely to occur. But spot checks can detect many of them. For example, the measuring devices used to distribute grains are usually tins that have been roughly cut and marked to use as scoops. Since the villagers have no way of knowing how much the scoops are supposed to measure or how to calculate the volume being dished out, it is possible for some food to be skimmed regularly at the distribution point. In remote areas, distribution teams may charge the local people for delivering and distributing food. People responsible for preparing distribution lists may demand a kickback for putting a family on the distribution roll. And, in some villages, food may be taxed by or voluntarily diverted to insurgents.

The most likely problem, however, is bogus recipients on the food rolls. Registration officials should be chosen for their honesty and thoroughly trained. During the registration process, spot checks by supervisors should be carried out wherever possible.

Choosing Foods for Programs in Lawless Areas

In areas where programs are plagued by banditry and looting of food supplies, agencies should carefully consider the foods they will try to supply. If the foods have become a target of thieves, it may be because they have high value on nearby markets. In Somalia in 1992, relief agencies imported rice, wheat, and vegetable oil for their famine feeding programs—commodities that more affluent Somalis favored in normal times. These foods also had long shelf lives, could be easily stored or hoarded for extended periods, had high value, were easily marketed outside Somalia, and were ideal food for soldiers. Since Somali money was virtually worthless, it was better to hold those foods than currency. When bandits realized relief agencies and political factions were powerless to stop or punish the looting, widespread attacks on relief shipments and stores occurred.

To stop the thefts, USAID, with the help of a few international relief agencies, decided on a two-pronged approach. They began by selling the higher-valued commodities to private traders to peddle in the markets at reasonable prices. Then they switched the foods in the free feeding programs over to lower-valued and less preferred commodities such as blended foods with a shorter shelf life and grains that the Somalis grew such as sorghum. The proceeds from the sales were used to fund cash-for-work projects organized by NGOs. They began by selling the higher-valued commodities to private traders to sell in markets at reasonable prices. The proceeds from the sales were used to fund cash-for-work projects organized by NGOs. (See previous discussion of the program, Chapter 7.) Then they switched the foods in the free feeding programs to lower-value and less preferred commodities such as blended foods with a shorter shelf live and grains that the Somalis grew, like sorghum.

The Somali program was successful, in large part because local merchants transported food through insecure areas into famine-affected regions. Local leaders and merchants had clan and religious affiliations and political and business relationships they used to take food into famine communities.

Controlling Price Fluctuations in the Peripheral Areas

The arrival of large numbers of displaced famine victims will probably increase food prices in the peripheral areas even though they may not have enough money or goods to purchase food for a sustained period. It usually will be necessary to intervene in the markets and initiate income-support projects to ensure the poor can buy food. As a rule, eligibility to participate in income-support projects should not be restricted to the displaced alone—rising food prices will affect the local poor as well.

Cash for work should be the primary approach. If people can buy food, area merchants will quickly bring more into the region to meet increased demand, thereby reducing the need for relief food. In many cases, this may be the fastest way to get food to the displaced. Indirect food-distribution programs such as food-coupon stores and food for work can also be initiated.

Afterword

Some Additional Thoughts About Famine

By Richard B. Hill

Starvation is the characteristic of some people not having enough food to eat. It is not the characteristic of there being not enough food to eat. While the latter can be a cause of the former, it is but one of the many possible causes. Whether and how starvation relates to food supply is a matter for factual investigation.

Food supply statements say things about a commodity considered on its own. Starvation statements are about the relationship of persons to the commodity. Leaving out the cases where a person may deliberately starve, starvation statements translate readily into statements of ownership of food by persons. In order to understand starvation, it is, therefore, necessary to go into the structure of ownership.

Amartya Sen
*Poverty and Famines:
An Essay on Entitlement and Deprivation*[1]

Experts often say the world's supply of food is adequate today to feed everyone—the problem is people's access to this food. The famine responder's task is to address this problem of access, so that some of the food gets to those who would otherwise starve.

At first glance, this is a logistics problem—the practitioner must find an efficient way to move food from wealthy, food-surplus-producing countries to regions where people are hungry. If food were free, this might be the famine responder's only task. But food is not free, and its cost becomes a greater issue every year. As foreign-assistance budgets shrink in developed countries, the supply of food—or, more correctly, the supply of money to buy food—will be reduced as well.

The responder's focus is now shifting from creating efficient food-transport-and-delivery logistics to devising mechanisms that look within famine-stricken societies for ways to supply enough food from local resources to make up the inevitable shortfalls of donor food assistance. In addition, famine responders may have to find ways to supply food to pockets of starvation within the society. These types of responses must be made early in the famine. If the famine is fully developed, it is too late to respond effectively.

In the twenty-first century, more and more emphasis will be placed on first detecting and mitigating incipient famine. When famine develops, we will try to find ways to fight it with local resources. This will be the challenge for those who respond to famine.

The preceding pages provide an outline of famine as it manifests itself in the late twentieth century, attempting to explain why there is famine and how we can do something about it. The responses discussed represent an array of techniques and programs developed in the field between 1972 and 1995. How can the famine responder use this information?

Responses to famine address prevention or mitigation of probable famines or provide relief to populations already affected by famine, either through conventional relief or counterfamine measures. In practice, the planner will find that an adequate response to famine can include most, if not all, of the procedures, mechanisms, programs, and operations discussed here. In areas where drought is endemic, the climatic, nutritional, and market early-warning programs, as well as logistics for food delivery, village and camp distribution procedures, food for work, cash for work, agricultural-rehabilitation programs and land-capacity analysis may all be required. Add a war, and all of these plus special security and counterconflict programs are likely to be a part of the range of responses. Comprehensive response to famine will use prevention and mitigation as well as conventional relief and counterfamine programs.

The planner must be aware of the links between politics, economics, patterns of culture, food supply, and the activities of international relief organizations and understand how and why these links are important. Furthermore, as the humanitarian-response community evolves, it generates new tools and responses that use technological advances and recent analysis of the links between food shortages and political and economic problems. All now become important in devising effective responses.

Prevention and Mitigation

Famine often occurs in cycles, so the response to one famine is linked to the efforts to prepare for the next. This is particularly true in dry climates, where drought or other climatic issues often trigger famine.

And in modern times, the responses to famines encouraged by well-meaning donor assistance and development agencies have sometimes become part of the dynamic that helps create another famine in following years.

This occurred, for example, in succeeding drought-induced famines in Somalia and other parts of the Sahel, where aid organizations drilled boreholes to tap aquifers to provide more water for animals and farms. This helps keep herds from dying and stabilizes prices for animals in the near term. But new boreholes and more water encouraged pastoralists to increase herds, placing ever-greater grazing pressure on fragile arid environments. As larger herds overgrazed lands adjacent to the new water points, they began to encroach on agricultural land and moved into areas where longstanding clan agreements had delineated boundaries for grazing. When rains failed, the large, stressed herds began to starve, and animals were dumped onto the market in large numbers, driving prices down. Food insecurity placed even greater pressure on clan relations, which had now grown rancorous due to disrupted grazing patterns and agreements, encouraging conflict, population displacements, further agricultural disruption, and food theft. In this and similar situations, criminals, violent power brokers, and warlords exploit the volatility of this situation. The next cycle of famine quickly begins.

In recent years, programs have been developed to provide early warning. The Famine Early-warning Systems discussed in Chapter 5 are designed to recognize the signs or components of an incipient famine and alert relief officials, so steps can be taken to provide agricultural assistance or food before crops are lost or populations begin migrating out of agricultural areas. These programs also often detect other environmental production problems such as plant disease or insect infestations. In recent years, some international organizations have attempted to provide political famine early warning by addressing political issues that have the potential to create war, isolate marginal agricultural areas, disrupt transfers of food, or otherwise contribute to famine. The United Nations Office for Coordination of Humanitarian Assistance (previously the Department of Humanitarian Affairs) provides reports on small wars and conflicts, population movements, and other economic and political problems that require a humanitarian response.

In addition, Fred Cuny helped form the International Crisis Group in 1994 to provide an independent analysis of potential humanitarian crises and their political, economic, and sociological causes and solutions. Cuny was a leader in the movement to think about solutions to these problems in a systemic way. He hated the idea that the relief community was responding to the same problems year after year in the same less-than-successful way. He wanted progress, and he realized that unless we found ways to influence elites and help them address the root causes of famines, we would continue to run in circles and respond to the same problems in the same places decade after decade. We are now witnessing some slow recognition of this in programs such as USAID's Greater Horn of Africa Initiative, which attempts to involve economics, the environment, and politics in regional systemic solutions to food insecurity.

At the other end of the crisis, an opportunity for mitigation is provided when a society comes out of a famine. At this point, attention to agricultural development can accelerate, and assistance can support those institutions that strengthen the local capacity for response and preparation for anticipated scarcity in coming years. There is at this point great potential for change. In the past, postfamine assistance sometimes followed the design of conventional-relief programs set up in the heat of the response, with emphasis on logistics and dependence on international organizations with reliable chains of supply and close relations with donors. For example, transport systems that operate parallel to local systems are often set up. These systems take on a life of their own, becoming an expensive duplicate system that continues to supply food and development supplies long after the emergency has passed. At the height of the famine, a system may have been set up to provide efficient transport where none existed. But it continues to exist for years as a competitor to economic activity in the recovering society.

When the emphasis remains on the use of international organizations and imported resources, those responses that use local resources, strengthen local organizations, support indigenous responses, or sustain creative local-coping strategies are less likely to receive assistance. Economic activity remains low, poor populations find it difficult to accumulate a resource cushion, and a society can easily cycle back into famine when food production is again disrupted.

We may find that turning to local resources in famine-stricken societies is essential for reasons other than helping societies recover. In the post-cold war era, most donors are reducing their relief and development assistance or finding that the amount available cannot cover the requirements of ever-larger emergencies. Because international assistance resources are constricting, the planner must move away from conventional relief programs and consider programs that use local resources. As planners and field managers are forced to find creative ways to maximize local resources and to support ingenious coping strategies for famines, they will strengthen both the capacities and resiliency in these populations. Thus this reduction of donor resources may also reduce the chance that famine will reoccur in subsequent years.

Conventional Relief and Counterfamine Relief

The bulk of the discussion in this book focused on providing some type of immediate relief to people affected by famine. Conventional relief attempts to directly attack the nutritional deficit by providing food to the hungry by a direct and efficient logistical method. Indeed, a massive international logistics operation may be the only way to save lives in severe situations, where early programs to contain the famine are inadequate or nonexistent.

The preceding chapters on nutrition and logistics will help guide the planner in designing effective responses for these conditions. But counterfamine measures provide assistance through systems that seek to avoid the replacement of local capacity with external capacities—a formula for dependency. A well-planned counterfamine measure may also build on a local capacity in a way that creates new social mechanisms to deal with the pressures of increased population or environmental degradation that contributes to recurrent famine. While logistical systems can be replicated from operation to operation, the design of a counterfamine program depends on a mix of economic, political, and environmental factors that have created the famine and are continuing to influence the dynamics of population movements, food delivery, agricultural activity, and other aspects.

This means that counterfamine measures cannot be standardized as well as conventional relief operations. The mix of conditions, which differ from famine to famine, dictates the options left open to the program planner at the time. The preceding pages will familiarize the planner with the range of choices, but these are based on past experience. The planner may develop an outline from these choices and suggestions, but successful famine response will require the planner to resist the easy solution—standard responses or a program used in previous years in another situation—simply because it is familiar and the implementation systems are worked out. An effective response that leaves the society better able to resist the slide into further food insecurity will require continued creativity by the program planner to use local structures to respond to changing situations with fewer donor resources.

As Amartya Sen points outs, famine is the set of problems that occur when there is no access to food. When environmental and logistics problems cause this lack of access, the relief community is better prepared to address famine then it was ten years ago. The tools available for combating famine have followed recent technological advances in information technology. More and better satellite data as well as advances in the analysis of this data have improved the ability to see drought, pest infestation, or the potential for crop-yield reduction due to environmental factors before large-scale food insecurity occurs. Techniques for transport and tracking relief commodities and responding to migrating populations have also improved with the use of better field communications and integrated databases.

For many years, famine responders have known that famine is a problem only partly tied to climate and transport logistics. Yet the solutions have usually been dominated by attention primarily to logistics and environmental solutions. After many years, policy makers and planners are beginning to design responses with the understanding that the cause of famine is tied as much to politics, markets, and local economics as to the environment and the logistics of moving food from rich countries to poor ones. The creation and exploitation of scarcity in a war economy, the effect of arms trading, the monopolization of resource access, and exploitative labor poles in starving societies are but a few of the important dynamics of famine in recent humanitarian responses.

These dynamics are complex. They create complicated problems that are not easily solved. In these new dynamics, the success or failure of the last agricultural crop may be relatively unimportant when compared to economic relations between elites and the manipulation of markets by wealthy traders. A region can have a good harvest, but famine occurs if conflict prevents food from getting to markets or to pockets of food deficit. In times of plenty, a famine cycle can begin if the market is oversupplied, driving prices so low that producers can not make enough to recapitalize, making them vulnerable to any production deficits in the following season. Poorly timed food assistance often contributes to this. Conversely, famine is averted in the midst of widespread crop failure if populations migrate to areas of adequate employment or there is a healthy system of alternative resources such as animals, savings, food banks, or diversified-income alternatives.

It is these economic relationships that now become a principle concern of the famine responder. And as these complex relations vary from society to society and from year to year within the same society, the famine responder may find that the response that worked well last year now prolongs the conflict and the famine.

These are not new phenomena. We have, in fact, been aware of these dynamics for many years. Sen published his *Poverty and Famines* in 1981, and he had been studying and writing about the relation between food and local economics for twenty years before that. As this book goes to press it has been announced that Sen is the recipient of a Nobel prize for economics — indication that mainstream academia has now understood the importance of the relationship between economics, access, and hunger. We can only hope the policy makers are not far behind.

Within the relief community, real understanding of these complex famine dynamics has only recently began to play a role in the definition of the problem and design of solutions. What is happening is a gradual shift in the way we organize our thinking about famine response. In years past, once a famine was in progress, the response was to provide food, and the formula was logistical. It is now more common for a planner to organize a response with programs that address political and economic issues. Logistical solutions to the provision of food are still important and will continue to be so—a famine response must improve nutrition, and bringing food to those who need it is still the most efficient way to do that. But logistics now become part of a complex economic and political dynamic that drives the famine.

The preceding pages should give the famine responder some idea of the range of strategies, approaches, and tools that have been used and can be used again to address famine. Fred Cuny attempted to simplify a complex subject—one for which simple solutions are usually inadequate. If used as a cookbook, the programs and approaches found here might be inadequate. If used as a guide to help the planner organize a creative approach to famine response, it may prove useful.

Notes

1. Copyright © 1981 International Labour Organization, Geneva. Published on behalf of the ILO by Clarendon Press, Oxford, by permission of Oxford University Press.

Bibliography

Berg, A. 1971. "Famine Contained: Notes and Lessons from the Bihar Experience." *Famine: A Symposium Dealing with Nutrition and Relief Operations in Time of Disaster,* Blix, G., Y. Hofvander, and B. Vahlquiest, editors. Uppsala: Swedish Nutrition Foundation, Symposium no. IX.

Bhandari M. 1974. "Famine Foods in the Rajasthan Desert." *Economic Botany* 28, no. 1.

Bureau for Refugee Programs. 1984. "Assessment of Displaced Persons Assistance Programs in El Salvador." Washington.

Cox, G. 1981. "The Ecology of Famine: An Overview." *Famine: Its Causes, Effects and Management,* J. Robson, editor. New York: Gordon & Breach Science Publishers.

Cuny, F. 1994. *Disasters and Development.* Dallas: Intertect Press.

———. 1988. "Paired Villages." Dallas: Intertect.

Currey, B. 1981. *Famine: Its Causes, Effects and Management,* J. Robson, editor. New York: Gordon & Breach Science Publishers.

Cutler, P. 1985. "The Use of Economic and Social Information in Famine Prediction and Response." A report prepared for the Overseas Development Administration.

Den Hartog, A. 1981. "Adjustment of Food Behavior During Famine." *Famine: Its Causes, Effects and Management,* J. Robson, editor. New York: Gordon & Breach Science Publishers.

Devereux, S. and R. Hay. 1986. *Origins of Famine: A Review of the Literature,* Volumes I and II. Paper prepared for Food Studies Group, Queen Elizabeth House. Oxford: University of Oxford.

de Waal, A. 1988. *Famine that Kills: Darfur 1984–85.* London: Save the Children Fund.

Hay, R. 1986. "Food Aid and Relief/Development Strategies." Paper presented at the World Food Programme-Asian Development Bank seminar, "Food Aid for Development in Sub-Saharan Africa." Abidjan.

Intertect. 1985. "Ethiopian Food Needs Assessment." For Catholic Relief Services, Baltimore.

Jackson, T. with D. Eade. 1982. *Against the Grain: The Dilemma of Project Food Aid.* Oxford: OXFAM.

Manetsch. T. 1981. "On Strategies and Programs for Coping with Large Scale Food Shortages." *Famine: Its Causes, Effects and Management*, J. Robson, editor. New York: Gordon & Breach Science Publishers.

Mayer, J. 1981. "Preface." *Famine: Its Causes, Effects and Management*, J. Robson, editor. New York: Gordon & Breach Science Publishers.

Seaman, J., J. Holt, and J. Rivers. 1974. *Hararghe Under Drought, A Survey of the Effects of Drought Upon Human Nutrition in Hararghe Province*. Addis Ababa: Ethiopian Government Relief and Rehabilitation Commission.

Sen, A. 1981. *Poverty and Famines: An Essay on Entitlement and Deprivation*. Oxford: Clarendon Press.

Stewart, F. 1982. "Poverty and Famines: Book Review." *Disasters 6*, no. 2.

Toole, M., R. W. Steketee, R. Waldman, and P. Nieburg. 1989. "Measles Prevention and Control in Emergency Settings." *World Health Organization Bulletin*.

USAID, Africa Bureau, Office of Sustainable Development, Crisis Management Response Division. *FEWS bulletin*. Arlington, VA: The FEWS Project.

Walker, P. 1987. *Famines: Family Warning and Preventative Action— The Need to Listen to the Victims*. London: International Institute for Environment and Development.

Wolde-Mariam, M. 1981. *Rural Vulnerability to Famine*. New Delhi: Vrikas Press.

Index

Kumarian Press is dedicated to publishing and distributing books and other media that will have a positive social and economic impact on the lives of peoples living in "Third World" conditions no matter where they live.

Kumarian Press publishes books about Global Issues and International Development, such as Peace and Conflict Resolution, Environmental Sustainability, Globalization, Nongovernmental Organizations, and Women and Gender.

To receive a complimentary catalog or to request writer's guidelines call or write:

Kumarian Press, Inc.
14 Oakwood Avenue
West Hartford, CT 06119-2127
U.S.A.

Inquiries: (860) 233-5895
Fax: (860) 233-6072
Order toll free: (800) 289-2664

e-mail: kpbooks@aol.com
Internet: www.kpbooks.com

Books of related interest from Kumarian Press

**The Challenge of Famine:
Recent Experience, Lessons
Learned**
John Osgood Field, editor

Famine is addressed within a framework of political economy. The central message is that planners must integrate famine policy with development policy.

US$19.95 / Paper: 1-56549-018-5

**Achieving Broad-Based
Sustainable Development:
Governance, Environment and
Growth With Equity**
James H. Weaver, Michael T. Rock,
Kenneth Kusterer

This comprehensive and multi-disciplinary work provides an excellent overview of economic development and the results of growth. The authors provide a model which looks through economic as well as social, political, and environmental lenses.

US$26.95 / Paper 1-56549-058-4
US$38.00 / Cloth 1-56549-059-2

**Reasons for Hope:
Instructive Experiences in
Rural Development**
Anirudh Krishna, Norman Uphoff,
Milton Esman, editors

Eighteen of the world's most exemplary rural development successes from Africa, Asia, and Latin America are presented in the words of their originators and managers.

US$19.95 / Paper: 1-56549-063-0
US$40.00 / Cloth: 1-56549-064-9

**Reasons for Success:
Learning from Instructive
Experiences in Rural
Development**
Norman Uphoff, Milton J. Esman,
Anirudh Krishna

Draws lessons from the accounts presented in Reasons for Hope. The book is enriched by the knowledge and insights the authors have gained from decades of participation, observation, and scholarship on Third World development.

US$19.95 / Paper: 1-56549-076-2
US$40.00 / Cloth: 1-56549-077-0

**Aiding Violence:
The Development Enterprise
in Rwanda**
Peter Uvin

This book explores the dramatic contradiction inherent in the existence of massive genocide in a country that was considered by western aid agencies to be a model of development. The processes of inequality, exclusion, and humiliation that have characterized social and economic life in Rwanda are considered and questions are raised about how development aid ignored and reinforced these characteristics of structural violence.

US$24.95 / Paper 1-56549-083-5
US$59.00 / Cloth 1-56549-084-3

**To order call Kumarian Press
1-800-289-2664**